House of Holy Fools
a family portrait in six cracked parts

by Amy Biancolli

TA DA! PUBLICATIONS   **LULU PRESS**
LuLu.com/amybiancolli

Published by Lulu Enterprises, Inc., 3131 RDV Center, Suite 210, Morrisville, NC, 27560.

Portions of Chapter 4 appeared in The Litchfield County Times and in *The Day My Father Died*, edited by Diana Ajjan, 1994 Running Press.

Page 25 photo by Sue Cheng. Page 93 photo by Louis Biancolli. Page 127 photo by Jeanne Biancolli. Title page and last page photos by Lucy Biancolli. The remaining photos that appear throughout the text are from the author's personal collection and are of vague or unknown origin. Credit, gratitude and apologies are hereby extended to the photographers, whoever they are.

Front cover illustration by Madeleine Ringwald
Back cover illustration by Jeanne Ringwald
Back cover author photo by Micaela Dingle

ISBN 1-4116-0444-X

For my living family:
Madeleine, Jeanne, Mitchell and Chris

And for Lucy, in the glorious elsewhere.

1

Lost and Found

Back then I figured death was obsessed with my family. He seemed to me an unwanted guest, oily and shrewd, with a stalker's bad personal hygiene and pants that gave him a wedgie. I would say death loomed over everything we said and did and saw, except that looming death is a repugnant cliché and anyway, it's wrong. Looming implies a spectral presence, a bogeyman frightening only in the least tangible sense. Shadows loom; fears loom; national malaise looms. As a child I never felt that death loomed. He was there, in the house with us, an irksome, malodorous visitor who claimed squatter's rights on the living room couch. All you had to do was round the corner and switch on the light and there he sat, his stocking feet on the cushions, his sticky fingers on a sandwich, his head cocked in raffish expectation. Up went his eyebrows when we glanced his way: C'mere, have a seat, he seemed to say. Been waiting for you all.

I hated the guy. I can't quite say he hated me back, but he certainly liked me less than any other member of my family -- he never sought my company the way he did everyone else's. I'm not sure why. But I always knew, even as a kid, even before I started to believe in crosses and burdens and curses and gifts, that I more than any other person in that damned and blessed house was doomed to survive. I say "doomed" (rhymes with "loomed") because no one knows better than the living the excruciating pains of death. I am alive -- I am well -- I am here to reflect on my parents' and sister's lives and deaths. I was given a gift massive in its beauties and responsibilities, and I was given it (I believe, I believe) the very moment I was born. I was burdened with health as my family grew sick and I was burdened with life as they died.

At times I've cursed them, and God, for leaving me here to sort through my grief and their histories. At times I've imagined joining them. But I can't -- I never could -- I'd be useless anywhere but here, in the hard mystery of the hard earth, where I have a family of my own to tether me. I know that I am needed. I know, too, that in some incomprehensible way Mama and Daddy and Lucy want or even need me to be here, to be well, to be alive, to move on with my own small doings, to recall and preserve their idiosyncrasies and find in their deaths some honest closure. They more than anyone gave me the tools to survive their absence; they more than anyone taught me to look at illness and loss and see not a ragged end but a beginning, clean and empty and open to the arrival of hope.

I glance at my younger daughter, dozing contentedly nearby. A smile shapes her lips and her face seems for a moment aglow with the person she will become. The person she already is -- she's in there, fully formed or near to it. That too I believe. And I believe that this child, like the child who came before her and the child who came after, is in a very real sense God's answer to my grief. I will never forget the sight of Jeanne's older sister, Madeleine, napping with similar contentment between the motionless legs of my mother on her deathbed. My mother, my daughter, my beginning, my end, resting together on the same cool white sheets in a large teaching hospital. Madeleine and Jeanne and their little brother, Mitchell, were all born one floor away. One exits; three arrive. Mama had two daughters. So do I. I move ahead, not retracing my mother's footsteps but making my own, crossing her path at some points, leaving it behind at others: She never had a son. I am determined not to relive my mother's life or her sorrows. While she lived I feared I might; her death reassures me that I needn't, can't, won't. "It's the end of a chapter," a friend told me shortly after Mama's death, which marked the passing of my entire childhood family. "Now it's time for the next one."

I am my family. I am not my family. I am not about to kill myself, as my sister did, as my father tried to. I will not carry on that legacy. As a girl I felt bound to my family and yet somehow apart, as profoundly and terrifyingly different as any child feels in a room full of towering strangers. It is hard to convey how deeply I loved them, how passionately I regarded their oddity and insanity and genius, how erratically I tilted toward them, then away, then toward them, then away. As a teenager I was loud in my anger and fell into clawing arguments with my mother, who recognized them for what they were -- a child's flailing grasps at control in uncontrollable circumstances -- and perhaps saw in me the family's one last chance at normalcy. I certainly was the closest it ever came to average. By an outsider's standards, I was manifestly eccentric, merely the youngest of the bona fide Biancolli oddballs who seemed always to be perched on the precipice of some new disaster -- medical, mental, financial -- and yet carried on, day after befuddled day, in a haze of music and mostly happy distraction. The Biancollis attracted misfortune and entertained death and knew both not intimately but in the mundanest and truest sense, as a child knows her classmates from the way they behave on the playground. She knows not what they think but how they act -- how fast they run, how klutzy they are, how badly they hog the ball. In that manner my family knew the habits of tragedy: they knew how it behaved, for it was a frequent visitor.

Death clumped often about our home. I knew this and responded to it very early in life, pondering the nature of non-existence with such earnest Weltschmertz that my parents nicknamed me "The Philosopher." None of us believed in God then -- Mama was agnostic, Daddy a committed atheist and former socialist -- so any random philosophizing about mortality was invariably filled with gloom (rhymes with "doom"). I remember sitting in the back seat of our navy-blue VW Squareback and staring out the window as my mother, always the driver in my family, tooled along the narrow bumpy road that circled the lake in Connecticut where I grew up. I was probably four years old. I was thinking hard about what it meant to die, to leave this world and not enter another one; the closest I could get to visualizing this was the thick dark horror of my bedroom at night. I feared the dark and slept with a light until I entered college.

Finally, abruptly, I shared this image with my parents. "When you die," I announced, "you don't see anything, you don't hear anything. There's nothing. It's all black."

Mama later told me that she was so stunned by this declaration that she pulled the car to the side of the road and stared, dumbfounded, at the existentialist peanut in the back seat. She swapped looks with my father. The Philosopher.

As it happened, black was my favorite color.

*****

This, then, is the story of my lost family. No, not lost: misplaced. I'll find them again someday, like those car keys I dropped in the kitchen closet or that shiny blue windbreaker I bought in Discovery Discount Fashions in 1983 and never wore again. They're around somewhere. I'll find them; I have to. And this is how.

When Mama lay dying in intensive care, I knew it and feared it and dreaded the dryness of the years I would spend without her. Madeleine was not yet eight months old. I sat in the hospital chapel and wept as my daughter gurgled and rolled around the room; her beauty, her joy, and her obliviousness to pain seemed an affront to my own faithless grief. Then a man entered and sat across the aisle from me. "Do you need to talk?" he asked. In reply I told him everything: how my mother had fallen, had struck her head on the sidewalk outside my home and now lay, comatose, as my husband and I awaited the results of her CT scan; how my father and sister had died two years earlier, the first of broken-hip complications, the second a suicide; how I mourned not just for my mother but for the relationship she might have had (indeed, already had) with my daughter. I looked at Madeleine, then turned to the man. "She'll never know my family," I said.

"Yes, she will," he told me. "Through you."

Through me.

At the time I did not believe him; I did not believe that I, surely the least consequential member in a family of idiosyncratic Titans, could convey to my children the vast landscape of Biancolli history, Biancolli weirdness, Biancolli lore. Yet here I am, pecking away at my laptop, hoping for all the world that my kids will one day grow up and read what I write. If they are to know Lucy and Mama and Daddy, they will know them through my words and memories and pictures framed with love. They will know them through this, this sentence collapsing upon this paragraph falling into that page of those chapters in this book. This tract filled with remembrance of anguish, illness, laughter, music, grace, arguments, clutter, books and death. This ode to dysfunction and function, madness and miracles. This sloppy memoir, tired dream, hopeful cant toward the next world from a pop-eyed glance at the past. This.

If autobiography is self-creation, then this small book is other-creation: I am creating not myself (not merely) but my dead family. They can be what I want and need them to be. In this sense my task is more fictive than non-fictive, as I am not simply describing the events of one and two and three and (good Lord is it now almost) four decades past. I am transforming them from fluid and messy human forms into neatly wrapped containers that hold in their tidy packaging every single characteristic that I care to remember (or, more to the point, memorialize). Those that I don't care to remember I will excise and chuck unceremoniously into the garbage. Snip, clip, toss. As the last living member of the household I exercise my right to bowdlerize and aggrandize as I see fit. Any friends or relatives with warring memories -- any folks who recall this peccadillo of my father's or that misguided passion of my mother's, and wonder why I've left it out -- I recognize as valid co-creators of the past and invite to write their own, wildly subjective versions of it. For any version of the past must be subjective, must be fictive, must be false. Honesty is for the living. And while I write this, I reside among the dead.

That I'll see them again someday is a given for me. I believe in a next world. I believe in a God. I believe that Lucy and Mama and Daddy are out there, bobbing in the netherworld, snapping their fingers to complex celestial rhythms. As I said before, they are misplaced. But did I ever really lose track of their whereabouts? Only in the sense that I can't lay my hands on them right away -- they don't come when I call them, or lick me when I whistle. They aren't, in other words, dogs. Yet I know where they are: I see them on the mantel in my living room, on the radiator in my bedroom, on the wall over the staircase landing, their flat eyes following me on my half-blind flits about the house. They're in my left ear as I cock it over Mama's violin (now mine) to hear the perfect fifth between the E and A strings. They're in my brown eyes, my belly laugh, and in the brown-eyed belly laughs of my three kids. They're in the newsprint on my hands, in the breadth of my hips, in my gifts for language and mimicry and in my love of words and film and music. In my fear of heights; my joy in movement; my headaches, temper, small hands, big feet, graying hair, loud voice and retro-New Deal George McGovern liberalism. I know where to find them because I find them in myself. In response to the question, "Can I escape these three tenacious and charismatic dead people?" the answer is, therefore, inevitably, No.

I love my family. I miss them and mourn them and wish they would leave me alone. I write this and wave at them in the remote and rapid flutter of a flat blue screen. They're here; as I write I say goodbye, as I'm destined to say goodbye, goodbye, and again, again, goodbye, until the day that I follow them, earning hushed farewells. In dying my parents and sister made of me a vessel harder and more enduring than any urn or coffin -- I carry them, all but their bodies, as no one else and nothing can. I'll hold their stubborn ether and shape it with my words long after my life is crammed with the stuff of other memories. Thus I part from them, now and always, casting off my family in an ever-final effort to shoo them irrevocably away. They'll never depart entirely -- but perhaps they'll reside elsewhere, somewhere nearby, somewhere in the imaginations of my children, who will enfold them in the unironic welcome of love removed by time. When my children finally own the ghosts of my family, when I have given them every created memory and told them every tale, then I will at last feel free to forget. And let them slip away.

I loved them; they left me.I love them still; and still, forever leaving, they remain.

2

Pill Hill

I grew up on a lake: Lake Waramaug, the second-largest natural lake in the Constitution State. Shaped like a Rorschach squiggle, the lake was named either a) after Chief Waramaug or b) for a Native American term that means "Good Fishing Place," depending on who's doing the etymology. It's about eight miles around and falls into three Connecticut municipalities, Kent, Warren and New Preston, the last being a village within the quaint and tony Litchfield County township of Washington. The Biancollis were neither quaint nor tony, but they were colorful, and New Englanders have always had a fondness for color, be it found in fall leaves or outlandishly dysfunctional families. The only thing about the Biancollis that qualified as monochromatic was the house itself, located on West Shore Road in the New Preston smidgen of the lake. A brisk twenty-minute walk brought you to the Washington

Town Beach and the southernmost point of the lake. Five minutes more brought you to downtown New Preston, a block-long business district (Main Street!) that stretched from the Boys Club at one end to the U.S. Post Office and Zinnicks' grocery (where the woman who ran it once shaved off a digit in the meat grinder, spooking me for the next ten years) at the other. In between were a package store, a gas station, a drug store, a hardware store, a barber shop, a lunch counter and a second, smaller grocery that my father, always walking, visited each day to buy the Daily News and a bag of Crystal Blue Mints. These he kept in a drawer at his bedside and sucked half-way before sticking them, perhaps for a rest, on the night table.

The house on the lake had ten and a half rooms: four bedrooms, two and a half bathrooms, a living room, a dining room, a kitchen, and a cramped downstairs guest room that doubled as a "music room" -- packed with orchestral scores, librettos, books about music, sheet music, music stands, and the ugliest-sounding upright piano that I have ever heard. I'm not sure why my parents hung on to that upright for as long as they did; it may have had something to do with the Mason & Hamlin concert grand sitting in the living room, which was worth more than any other single item in that house and which my mother tried valiantly to protect from my father's untrained hands. Banned from the grand, Daddy banged away at the upright, producing intergalactic chords that had no clear relation to what are generally recognized as the elements of Western harmony. He played the piano and accordion by ear, or tried to. The latter instrument he lugged down to our boat house (no boat) whenever he wanted to squeeze out a tune, thoughtfully protecting his family's delicate ears from the resultant squeaks and wows but guaranteeing that everything he played would be heard, clear as glass, by everyone who lived across the lake. Daddy was nothing if not considerate.

My mother was obsessed with home improvement. I say this not to suggest that she was a bouffanted

homemaker on a tear through back issues of House
Beautiful but to convey her profoundest faith in the Do
This Thy Self credo formed and nurtured during her Great
Depression upbringing. When Mama married Daddy she
also married roughly 5,000 hard cover books, which wasn't
a problem when they were living in a small Queens flat
(because all the books were in storage), but it became a
problem when we all moved into Daddy's old summer
home in Connecticut (because my parents were then
obliged to unpack every last book and find for it
accommodating shelf space). So Mama made bookshelves.
Everywhere. In the living room, the dining room, the
corridors, the bedrooms, the staircase -- if it had walls, it
had bookshelves. Even one of the bathrooms, if my
memory isn't playing tricks on me (or if I'm not playing
tricks on my memory), had a bookshelf at one point,
although I think it was removed when the books there
located started to mold. Most of the books shelved in that
old house I never laid a finger on, but they were essential
fixtures of the household, like the ceilings or window
sashes. There were volumes upon volumes of literary
masterpieces (complete sets of Dickens, Conrad, Austen,
Shakespeare), old socialist tracts, histories, music
encyclopedias, maps, biographies of obscure historical
figures, books on philosophy, science books for lay
readers, anatomy books, thesauri and grammars and
dictionaries for the study of Lithuanian and Latvian and
Swahili and Ancient Greek and Modern Greek and New
Testament Greek and Latin and Polish and Spanish and
Portuguese and Hebrew and Sanskrit and Russian and
French and German and a zillion other languages, and
there were translations of the Bible in every one of them.
Daddy always studied the Bible, not because he believed it
but because it was the one book published in every
language he cared to study. He ordered Bibles through the
mail and pored over them with a magnifying glass, cross-
referencing cognates and thumbing through fat
etymological reference books. You could hardly sit in that

house without putting one of your cheeks on a dictionary.

So Mama made bookshelves. She made porch steps to replace four that rotted. With the help of a how-to plumbing book and a friendly young hardware salesman she installed a shower, actually a dribble, into the upstairs bathtub. In my senior year of college Mama phoned to inform me that she had painted most of the living room orange. And she did mean orange. When the living room sofa wore out she disassembled it and rebuilt it as a spartan wood settee, complete with spindled back, severe brown cushions and orange trim. She also made what proved to be the most permanent monument to her ambitious spirit, a giant cement stair (singular) lined with stones that was supposed to be the uppermost step in a grand approach to our home but was quickly orphaned when the work became too back-breaking and Mama abandoned it. Somewhere I've got a photograph of Mama working on that step, her socks around her ankles, her right hand clutching a hose, a heavy shovel lying in the mud beside her. So proud was she of her single, huge stair and the herculean work that went into it that when my parents finally decided to have a blacktop driveway paved all the way up to the front of the house she instructed the workers not to dig up her lovingly laid creation. The step remained, a firm reminder of Mama's Brobdignagian effort.

The house sat on about an acre of land. On the front lawn grew two large sugar maples, one Japanese dwarf red maple, two birch trees, two weeping willows and a large assortment of shrubs. In the side garden were day lilies and a couple of rose bushes. Out back were impatiens and more roses and daisies and the biggest, most sumptuously leafy Norwegian maple tree in southern New England. Mama had a green thumb and felt so deeply for vegetable matter that the mere sight of a wilting plant (in a friend's home, a department store, a supermarket) sent her on an immediate and fervid rescue mission. She loved plants and was flummoxed by negligent dolts who allowed them to die. (I, being negligent, did most of the flummoxing.) Three years after Mama died -- four years after she moved, newly widowed, into a one-story pre-fab in Millerton, New York -- I finally screwed up the courage to visit the old house. It had been purchased by a successful developer and his wife; they had landscaped, carved out a new driveway, dug up the willows in front and installed a swimming pool in back. At first sight I couldn't spot Mama's red dwarf maple and feared it'd been sacrificed. It wasn't: the new owners had simply moved it off to the side. So great was my relief upon learning this that I stopped just short of flinging my arms around the man's neck and weeping full-slobber onto his chest. I'll never forget Mama's proud puttering over that squat maple, just as I'll never forget the sight of her on her knees in the garden, her fair round face pink with exhaustion. As my father used to say, What a Dame.

(Daddy said other things. He said, Jeannie, You Are a Goddess. He said, Girls, Isn't Your Mother a Goddess? He said, Jeannie, I Worship You. I Worship You, Jeannie. To which Mama replied -- later on, after such things mattered to her -- "Don't worship me! Worship God!" To which Daddy provided a nonverbal nasopharyngeal response, roughly transliterated as "Neeeeeeeeiiiahhhhh," followed by a melodramatic stinky-diaper grimace and the vague observation that "I leave that stuff alone." Meaning not stinky diapers but, of course, God. And he did leave God alone, except when he was deifying Mama or studying a translation of the New Testament or instructing a pimply bagger at Morey's IGA in the exact Swahili translation of "God bless you." Daddy liked to bless people, but it never occurred to him that he might actually be invoking God every time he did it. He was much more comfortable invoking Mama. Jeannie, You're The Most Beautiful Woman in the World! I'd Be Lost Without You! Oh, My Jeannie! What a Dame!)

The neighbors admired Mama's handiwork in the garden, but they didn't admire her other work around the house, because there wasn't any. As a child I routinely broke windows (using basketballs, baseballs, soccer balls, lacrosse balls, Frisbees) and Mama routinely boarded them up, having no money then or later to replace the glass. Similar lack of funds accounted for the house's wan gray color, actually a coat of white lead paint that had been applied circa 1948 and had, as far as I was aware, never been touched up. For more paranoid reasons, Daddy and Mama resolved when Lucy and I were toddlers not to mow the bottom half of the lawn, believing knee-high grass would dissuade us two whippersnappers from barreling all the way down the hill and into traffic (excuse me: I meant "traffic"). They were equally anxious about the porch, the back half of which hung over a one-story drop to the old driveway. Fearing their little ones would pole vault over the porch rails and plunge to their deaths below, they encased the entire wrap-around porch in chicken wire. This remained until shortly before my 28th birthday.

The house was never winterized -- despite cold that froze the lake until a Beetle could cross it, despite snow that piled up so high, one winter, that Daddy shoveled out through a first-floor window. It was built following World War I by Colonel Jackson, a man I know nothing about but always pictured with a pointy white beard and bolo tie, probably because I ate too much Kentucky Fried Chicken in my youth. He built our house and two neighbors' houses, the smaller of which began life as a carriage house for the larger. In the 1950s my father and his first wife got wind of a sweet real estate deal and snapped up a few houses around this wriggling worm of a lake in Connecticut. I suppose they thought they'd sell them all and make a bundle. They did not. This left my poor absent-minded impractical un-businesslike money-loathing father with several nice vacation homes and property taxes he could not afford to pay. He dumped all but one, which became our home; the others included that second Colonel Jackson house, a massive white Colonial with a commodious front lawn. Mama and I always ribbed Daddy for selling that house and keeping ours. But I never really wanted to live there; it was too beautiful. Though the family it housed was gracious and unfailingly kind, the building itself seemed foreign to me, its blazing-white clapboards and gorgeously appointed interior so far removed from our untidy reality.

The Biancolli manse was the sloppiest in the neighborhood. Earlier in her marriage and my life Mama kept a clean house, but later on a series of fairly spectacular medical catastrophes left her less inclined to hunch over linoleum with a toothbrush. Her cleaning and ours thereafter became pointedly event-oriented: After allowing layers of crap (thatches, laundry, papers, dust) to accrete to crisis levels throughout the house, and after learning that advancing forces of Neat People (relatives, pupils, neighbors, friends) were about to enter our home, we launched into an extended cleaning frenzy the likes of which no outsider can truly fully appreciate. Try to imagine eight-hour microsurgery performed by a team of surgeons. Now try to imagine those same surgeons using Lemon Pledge to get honey stains off of a piano bench.

I feel guilty about divulging such dirty little secrets, because I know how embarrassed Mama would have been to know that her youngest daughter has chosen to publicize her Dear Dead Mother's variegated housekeeping foibles. In her heart of hearts, my mother did not want to be a slob; she was not proud of being a slob; she wished, for all the world, that she were not. But events plotted against her, drained her time and her energy, made her use all of her free time -- what little she had -- on cryptograms, murder mysteries and "Magnum, P.I." She took care of a senile husband 24 hours a day, so she had a right. As it was she bathed regularly and cooked creative low-salt meals and washed the dishes every other day or so and mopped and swept now and then and did the laundry when absolutely necessary. Sometimes when she did the laundry she hung it out to dry and then gathered it up and placed lumps of it at various points throughout the house (the snug chair up against the staircase was a favorite spot, as was the glider-rocker in the upstairs hall), remaining in their designated waiting points until the stacks were depleted, piece by humble piece, as members of the family required fresh clothing. Sometimes, I'm not sure why or how, the Great Laundry Lumps were moved en masse into Mama's cavernous bedroom, where Mama spent very little time but which became a lost-sock-and-pillowcase headquarters for the entire house, a control room where Captain Mom and her Giant Mass of Clothing oversaw every piece of cotton, wool, silk, blend or polyester fabric that had not survived the arduous trek to a drawer. These forlorn items piled up and up and up until hillocks of cloth occupied every square inch of the bed and floor space. Merely opening the door to the room became difficult after a while, so jammed it was with abandoned t-shirts and vintage 1973 elephant pants. Every now and then I have a vision of some multicolored toe-sock I owned as a child, and I imagine it's still alive, somewhere, its vibrant polyester weave capping Mama's everlasting laundry heap in the sky.

One of the two upstairs bathrooms, the one we called the Grownups' Bathroom (the other, situated between Lucy's room and mine, was the Children's Bathroom), was filled with sundry junk -- boxes crammed with papers, old cleaning supplies, brooms, hand creams, forgotten and broken knickknacks, cheap novels and self-help guides that no one cared enough about to shelve. The toilet was inaccessible, the bathtub was packed with stuff, but it didn't matter; the pipes in there had busted, and my parents never bothered to get them fixed. Again, they didn't have the money.

The problem, when I think on it, is that Mama and Daddy never used the attic. There was one, of course. There was a trap door in the ceiling of the hall, and I remember Mama climbing up there once -- *once* -- to do who knew what. Successive generations of mice and squirrels lived in the attic and in the walls of the house, so maybe she was setting a trap. Resident animal life might have been one reason Mama and Daddy never ventured there again (fear of rabies? beaver fever? small, razor teeth?); that, or perhaps they thought the attic floors were weak and figured one their children, helpless schlemiels that they were, might fall through. Imagine my amazement when the house's new owner treated me to a tour of the attic and I didn't break my neck. It was my first time up there, and I felt naughty: I was breaking my parents' rules, shattering their world schema. As far as I'd known, as far as they'd taught me, Colonel Jackson's aging structure had no functioning storage space beyond Mama's bedroom and one small john. Those wacky Biancollis! Always pretending there wasn't an attic, when all the time there was!

Life as a Biancolli: It meant piles of things. My closet and Lucy's were jammed to capacity with frayed clothing and toys we hadn't touched since toddlerhood. Our rooms burst with burgeoning book collections of our own -- Lucy's (when she was older and veering toward God) had lots of brainy C.S. Lewis books, fuzzy spiritual studies, music theory texts and slim French masterworks. My shelves carried a heavier load of kitsch: "Star Trek" novels, "Star Trek" magazines, "Star Trek" histories, "Star Trek" short story collections, "Star Trek" encyclopedias and blueprints and compendia and concordances and puzzle books and quiz books and photonovels and biographies and convention memoirs and technical manuals. I had a drooling crush on William Shatner and owned any published material that concerned him, or at least his face. Plus I owned a bunch of Agatha Christie books, many of them hand-me-downs from my parents (Daddy gave me my first Hercule Poirot, *The Murder of Roger Ackroyd*). And Rex Stouts -- that is, Nero Wolfes (Wolves?). And Tarzans and Sherlock Holmeses and Harriets the Spy and Pippi Longstockingses and any other book or series of books featuring either plucky girls or manly men. I had a crush on Tarzan. Not the movie

Tarzan, I mean the book Tarzan; I liked the way Edgar Rice Burroughs described his muscles. Probably because of his mustache I also had a crush on Charlie Chaplin, whose glum mug was up there on my bedroom wall for years along with portraits of Captain Kirk, Jack Nicklaus (no crush, just a weird golf thing) and assorted Kliban cats. For some reason I never tacked up a photo of The Six Million Dollar Man, but he, too, was high on my list. (Why? she asks herself, many years later. Was it the sideburns? Was it the squint? Why?)

Except for a six-foot poster of Clark Gable that I bought and gave to her so that I, not she, could see it hanging in her bedroom, Lucy never had any Guys on her wall. I suppose it's because she rarely had crushes on celebrities -- she had intense infatuations and suffered madly through them, but they usually involved a kid from class (Kenny Ernhaut, first grade) or a science teacher (Mr. Yovan, seventh grade;- I had the hots for him, too) or some other ambulatory Y chromosome who entered her world on a regular basis. Thus Lucy never or rarely had photos of her crushees, which meant she had plenty of wall space for more highfalutin purposes: things she had written and was proud of, pretty pictures of flowers or animals, tiny funny portraits she had drawn of the characters peopling her fantasy world, the court of King Herman. Lucy's room was neater than mine and displayed a much finer intelligence at work there. I was a dumb galoot by comparison.

The two other upstairs bedrooms were Mama's and Daddy's. They had separate bedrooms -- not from lack of sexual interest but because Daddy, my dear, sweet, totally bananas Daddy, could not sleep with another human body in bed with him. I have no idea where this neurosis came from, but it was a fact, and Mama learned to live with it. Daddy's bedroom was no bigger than Mama's but it felt bigger because it lacked the lava-like cover of garments. For many years and for no reason I ever ascertained the only picture that hung on his wall was a print of a Van Gogh, a warm study of a bedroom bathed in sunlight.

When I was nine or ten I gave him a spin-art poster that I'd done at the Bridgewater County Fair, and he hung its darting blues and reds and yellows on the wall above his bed. It went surprisingly well with the Van Gogh. Beyond those two works of fine art Daddy's room was decorated with books, which gathered in stacks on the floor and stretched to the ceiling in two large bookshelves, and with two heavy manual typewriters -- one black, one charcoal gray -- that anchored a blunt pine table along the room's east side. Beneath it sat a wooden box brimming with magenta typing paper and Reader's Digest letterhead, which my Uncle Freddie mailed to us from his job at the magazine. As a girl I often sat at one of Daddy's typewriters and produced oblique childish sagas involving hikes through the woods and the acquisition of many large toys.

The downstairs of the house was more or less swallowed whole by Lucy's piano, purchased after she turned thirteen and had announced her intention to become a soloist. The Mason & Hamlin was a monster of an instrument, a graceful hulk of iron and wood that produced a sound as warm and soft as fresh-baked bread. Under Lucy's hands the instrument spoke, as my mother's violin spoke, as my father's words spoke from the top sheet of a typing carbon. Lucy was born to play the piano; she knew that, and embraced it joyfully.

I recall that piano as vividly as I do my family's old thick-legged dinner table (which sits at this moment in my own dining room), or the purplish sofa with enormous nubbly pillows that sent forth clouds of dust whenever someone sat on it (which doesn't). That poor puce creature died a merciful death while I was in junior high. It sat in the living room, its back to the piano, its front facing the fireplace, its worn arms extended in invitation to my father, who never accepted. Instead he sat in a torn white overstuffed Naugahyde chair with fake brass buttons, a piece of furniture that was if possible even more hideous than the couch and which stood on brown legs, splay-footed like an old man's, before a pair of tall French doors. Daddy sat in that chair and did crossword puzzles. Sometimes he sat just to talk to me or Mama (me with my homework, Mama with her crosswords) or to listen to Lucy, whose hours-long pummeling at the piano wafted through the house and down the hill and over the trees to the neighbors' homes. So much of Lucy's playing I heard at a distance, from my hideout in the back-yard saplings, from the Adamses' cottage on the waterfront, from my "house" in the hedge that separated our property from the Duuses', from the hut high up in the woods where my friend Sharon and I played and fought with her brothers and sister and built crazy fires that singed my bangs. Tucking me into bed one night Mama sniffed the smoke on me and asked if I'd built a fire and I said no and Mama said nothing but I knew she knew I had lied. I never knew why Mama said nothing, and I can't ask her now. But how clearly I feel my corduroyed bottom against the cold dirt floor of the clubhouse. How clearly I hear Lucy's music, faint yet unmistakable, shushing like breath through the trees.

The house of my childhood was filled with music -- Lucy's, Daddy's, Mama's, mine. Mine was the least of the four; Mama always said I had more raw talent than anyone in the family, but I never believed her. I took violin lessons and tried hard not to practice. How could I, with Mama, the Mother of all violin teachers, pretending to ignore me upstairs? She was my instructor for the first few years of lessons, but gave up when the stress of it freaked us both out. It was too much -- I felt the squeeze of expectation, despite the fact that Mama never pressured me, never pushed -- so she hooked me up with one of her star high school pupils (Janna; I liked her), who taught me until I quit at 13. I went back to the fiddle 13 years later, but that's another story.

When loved ones die, they become, for the bereaved, a collection of odd details -- as though by dying their wholeness shatters into a million scattered pieces. I can no longer hug Mama and Daddy and Lucy, so I hug their earthly afterthoughts: Mama's wind chimes, Daddy's magnifying glass, Lucy's spotted-hyena earrings, carved from balsa. For a year after my mother's death I hung on to her ratty old Dell puzzle books, two dozen of which were stacked punctiliously on a bedroom shelf. They mattered to me only because they mattered to her, only because she had filled out the crosswords and cryptograms in pen (more of a challenge), only because I would never again see her in the dim light of the living room, glaring down her nose at a page filled with words and checkerboard boxes. Death forces meaning upon the smallest bits of life. Why else do I shut my eyes and conjure every particle of that mad and loving house? Why else do I hear Lucy's etudes, Daddy's grumbling protests, Mama's early-morning fiddles in the music room? Why else do they reside there, now as then, now as always? Why else would I mourn the passing of a building, a mere structure with flaked paint and sagging floorboards, much as I mourn the passing of its mortal contents?

The fact is, I was passionate about that house. We all were. Daddy called it Pill Hill and Medicine Square Garden, both references to the family's vast pharmaceutical intake. The rest of us called it nothing in particular other than home, never bestowing upon it a cutiepie nickname like The Maples or The Waterfront or The Overlook or The Massive Yawning Maw of Death (Abandon All Whatever). Not that we didn't assign cutiepie nicknames to other objects and aspects of our lives. The Norway maple I mentioned was known as "Sweetheart" -- Lucy embraced it and kissed it regularly. (I hung a tire under it and swung on it. My own kiss of sorts.) To the side of the house wound an old recessed driveway that cut into and under the hillock on which the house rested. No longer used as a driveway, it became "the gully," a dump for garden waste and coal ashes and other assorted dross that Mama didn't feel like lugging to the town landfill. I never dwelled on this oddity -- the wisdom of maintaining a private dump for the disposal of twigs was never questioned -- and indeed didn't give it a thought until I described the house and property to a disbelieving college friend. Why did we have a gully alongside the house? she wanted to know. Why would my parents need a place to dump ashes and lawn refuse? Geez, I said. I didn't know. Why wouldn't they?

Such moments of befuddled realization dotted my upbringing, windows into the fertile absurdity of my home. The music room, for instance: Didn't everyone have a room in their house that smelled like crumbling sheet music? Didn't everyone have a cat that weighed twenty pounds (Peter; Maine Coon), a house that hadn't been painted in decades, a porch encased in chicken wire and a lawn that wore a beard of two-foot grass? When I was young, I felt overwhelmed by oddballs. My family embarrassed me. How to explain to squinty-eyed peers why my strange old father wore a beret every day, morning to midnight, all the time? How to explain his age (56 when I was born), his early retirement, his way-beyond-neurotic obsessions with my safety, his arm-twirling Swedish calisthenics as he walked along the road? He looked like a windmill. Of course I was embarrassed.

I knew enough about myself to spot my own distinctiveness, long before I was old enough to celebrate it. From age ten onward I felt like an old woman trapped in a child's body, as though there would never be, for me, a youth or young adulthood. As I grew through my teenage and college years I felt less trapped in my skin than simply at odds with my chronological age: I felt not nineteen or twenty, but eight and eighty-six. I was very young and very old simultaneously. Even now I sense disagreement between my accumulated birthdays and my concomitant feelings of childishness and advanced age. I peer at my image and marvel at newborn wrinkles, seeing in their cracked arrival the confirmation of my own long-held belief; yet I need only shut my eyes to see past that image to another one, an apple-cheeked girl in a bathroom mirror. Mama liked to say that when she glanced at her reflection she half expected to find a thirty-year-old woman gazing back at her. Perhaps, when I'm sixty-five, I'll expect the same.

Or not: Thirty was a strange for me. At twenty-eight I lost my sister, then my father. At twenty-nine I lost my childhood home. At thirty I lost my mother and my husband lost his father. So furiously did loved ones depart in those few years that I grew wary of arrivals; with the anguished love of a new mother I feared I'd lose my first child (then my second, and now my third), knowing all too well the random swing of the door between life and death. It is a sudden passage.

I forget, sometimes, how old I actually am. I forget how many years I spent in that house on the lake. I forget Mama's birthday, or how old Lucy was when she died, or the year Mama and Daddy got married. I'm no good with dates and sometimes count the years on my fingers. But it doesn't matter -- the virtue of writing, the virtue of memory, is the shading it throws on secondary details. What matters is not the age of the house but the speckled black linoleum on the tacky kitchen floor; not the year Lucy was born but the Snow White purity of her skin; not the date of my parents' anniversary but the warm moist *shhtwich* of their kiss. These things I remember; these I can record. The rest is less than history.

One day, greeting my oldest daughter on her return from pre-school, I bent to kiss her head. Her hair smelled of sweet white construction paste. "You smell like school," I told her. But what I meant to say was: You smell like childhood. You smell like everything I smelled, everything I knew and felt and heard and saw and ate and made and dreamed, when I was a round-faced girl. When I was a round-faced girl.

Sometimes, lying in bed at night, I visit them. They're back now, all of them, Mama and Daddy and

Lucy. They're in the house on Waramaug. Mama's asleep in the living room, stretched out on the sofa with an overweight cat on her chest. Lucy's in the kitchen with a mug of tea. Daddy sits opposite her, cracking mints between his teeth, his long, elegant fingers stroking the pages of a thin Icelandic grammar. From outside comes the distant whine of a buzz saw, a snarly harbinger of winter's end. It's early March; the snow outside has turned to mud; the last rays of late-afternoon sunlight spike the kitchen.

Sometimes I picture them at the kitchen table, passing around bottled vitamins and cartons of whole milk. Sometimes they're opening presents on Christmas morning. Most of all I imagine driving up to the house late on a summer night, my husband in the front passenger seat, my kids snoozing in the back. I imagine pulling up to the front porch; a single bare bulb is crowded with gnats and moths. As my husband and I persuade our groggy children from the car, my mother emerges from the house to greet us. We hug her. She hugs the kids and tells me how beautiful they are. Inside I find Lucy at the piano. She jumps up and throws her arms around my neck and rocks, left foot to right foot to left. God I missed you, Ame. Good to see you. Daddy clumps down the stairs and gives us a startled, happy look. Amy! I didn't expect you! And say, who's this handsome man with you! – he shakes my husband's hand, grabs his arm. Quite a bicep!

I've got some supper for you, Mama says.

Mama it's okay we ate, I say.

No, I've got supper for you, come on.

In the kitchen Mama gives us plates full of London broil and stuffed peppers. For the kids she brings out hot dogs – Oh, they smell good, wish I could eat That Salt – and absurdly tall glasses of chocolate milk. The girls make goofy faces at Lucy and Lucy makes goofy faces back. You kids used to do that at supper time, drove me nuts, Mama says. Lucy makes a goofy face at Mama. The children giggle. Daddy remarks on their thick hair and dark eyes – Say, they do look Italian, don't they, he says. Yes,

Daddy. Italian and German and Irish and EnglishScottishFrench. Irish? Who's Irish? Daddy asks. I am, Chris says, Irish and German. Ah! Sprechen Sie Deutsch? says Daddy. Ja, ja, ein bisschen, says Chris. You're ready for more London broil, Mama tells me. No, Mama, really, I'm fine. Here, I'll get you a small piece. No, Mama. Yes, here you go, a small piece. I'm full, Mama. Here, you've been driving all night. But I don't want more, Mama, I'll explode. You've been driving all night. You've been driving all night. Eat.

I do as she says. I wash my dish with a stack, always a stack, of old ones in the busy metal sink beside the washer. I say good night and hug everyone, long hard hugs, not stiff perfunctory dah-link hugs that say Yes Okay See You In The Morning, for I will not see them in the morning, I will never again see them in the morning. I watch as my children smack tickling kisses against their cheeks. In my father's eyes I see amazement. In my mother's I see gratitude. In my sister's, relief. I smile at them, hug them again, then turn my back to them and gently nudge my children from the kitchen. My husband and I take them upstairs. I put the kids to bed in my old room, a willow tick-tacking against the panes. And as I sit in the dark beside them, I hear the muffle of kitchen voices from below, distant trickles of colloquy and laughter.

3

Lucy Goosey

Lucy was the first to die, so I'll begin with her end. Daddy's death makes no sense without Lucy's, Mama's none without Daddy's. A led to B led to C, bim bam boom, a billiard ball kissing the edges of a table or a snake of sleek black dominoes felling each other, piece by piece. One death followed another so neatly and naturally that I can't imagine the three of them dying out of turn, say, Mama then Daddy then Lucy; to shuffle the order would seem rude, vulgar, like a pushy shopper butting into line at the grocery store. Hey, lady. Waitcher turn.

So Lucy stays up front, where she belongs. She was thirty-one when she died: on a Saturday, in early April, 1992. She downed lime seltzer with a big old bunch of pills -- anti-depressants, anti-convulsants, relaxants, even a couple anti-psychotics -- and curled up in a fetal position on her bed in an ample subsidized apartment in Cambridge, Massachusetts. After arriving at Lucy's place for the funeral Mama and Chris and I found a dark, thick residue inside the toilet bowl and on the chest fur of a fuzzy polar bear named Julien, after *The Red and The Black*'s randy hero. We cleaned up the gunk without asking what it was, but I always assumed it was either bile or dried blood -- proof that Lucy vomited, badly and probably painfully, before she died. And yet her lifeless face, sweet with hope, reflected not anguish but the warm light of expected peace.

I didn't see her dead. Lucy's friend Tamar found her, after phoning frantically Saturday night and Sunday in the slim hope she'd answer. Believing Lucy was at home, or should have been, and knowing that she had slid into the lowest underbelly of depression, Tamar finally phoned for help and entered Lucy's place with the police. In the bedroom she discovered Lucy's silent body, curled like a sleeping child.

I won't feel guilty that I wasn't around the weekend Lucy killed herself; I won't feel guilty that Chris and I flew out of town without leaving her a phone number (without even telling her we'd be gone); I won't feel guilty because Tamar and I and Mama and God knows who else couldn't or didn't answer the phone that Saturday, because Lucy's incessant neediness had started to bug me, or because the severity of her illness had, by the end, pushed her past anyone's ability to help. "I might be crazy, Ame," she said to me, about a month before she died. "You know, maybe I'm crazy. But I don't think I am." She was: The madness that overtook her, the hallucinatory and paranoid urgency of her last, bewildered interactions with friends and family, lent a stiff inevitability to her suicide. When her illness killed her grasp on reality, it killed her, too. There was nothing left for her but the irrefutable fact of death.

*****

Lucy was an unconventionally beautiful woman: five feet three and a half inches tall, with black Brillo hair, translucent skin and colossal, perfectly round violety-blue eyes. As a thirteen-year-old she was all elbows and twiggy knees and metal apparatus – braces on her teeth, earrings in her ears, blockish, metal-framed glasses to combat myopia – but high-school ballet lessons and a burgeoning appetite added weight to her figure and lent a seraphic pudginess to her face. As an adult she never looked her age; people always thought I was the older sister, by far.

But Lucy rarely felt confident about her looks and had a hard time believing she was anything any man would ever bother looking at. She ached to find romantic love. I tried to reassure her. I told her she was beautiful and told her she deserved love and told her she would find love and told her she was a gem, a catch, a rare find, and told her that she was wonderful and compassionate and hilarious and intelligent and great company and gorgeous, yes, gorgeous, yes, Lucy, I did say gorgeous, and told her lots of guys had had crushes on her (it was true) and told her she'd be married someday and told her God wanted her to be happy and told her God would make her well and told her that I believed everything I had told her, especially that last bit about God wanting her to be happy and making her well, even though I wasn't sure of that myself. I told her. Over and over and over, I told her. "Am I human, Ame?" she'd ask. "Am I human? I don't feel human." And I'd say yes. Yes, Lucy. Yesyesyesyesyesyesyes. You Are A Live Human Being. No You Are Not a Monster. Yes You Have a Right to Tell Your Shrink He's Full of Crapola. No He Will Not Press The "Eject" Button and Send You Flying Over the Suburbs of Boston. No You Are Not A Repulsive Worm. No. Yes. No. Yes. Whatever she needed me to say, I said it for her; I once drew "NO" on my face in black magic marker, which at least cheered her up for fifteen minutes.

I used to think that I could make her happy. I used to think that I could make her well. I used to think that if I prayed hard enough, said the right Novena in the proper frame of mind through the properly plugged-in intermediaries (the stigmatist Padre Pio, who pulled off bilocation, devil-boxing and numerous other hyper-saintly feats during his lifetime, was a particular favorite of mine), God would hear me, wake up, snap open those big lazy eyes of His and say (yawning), "Eh? What's that I hear? Lucy's sick? Dang. I'll just wave this Mega-Super-Blaster-Divine-Pixie-Dust right here and make her well. Whoops! Spilled some! But this oughta do it. Here goes!" Then, Zap. Lucy would be alive and well and concertizing and living in Des Moines with a loving husband and three darling children and a cat named Fred, or Dmitri, or something. That God might not want Lucy to be alive and well didn't actually occur to me until after she had died, when I was forced to confront the cruelest mystery of a believer's relationship with the Almighty: That He might have helped, and didn't. If I loved Lucy so much, if everyone on this ratty little planet desired for her only joy, why didn't God want the same? How could God love Lucy yet sit back, hands idle at His sides, while she got sicker and sicker? "Why do you choose me as your target?" asked Job, and Lucy wondered the same thing, aloud. I wondered the same thing for her.

Shortly after Lucy died, a well-meaning friend tried to console me by declaring that suicide isn't actually senseless, that it's really just an individual's informed choice to end one life and move on to a better one: you know, like upgrading a stereo system when the sub-woofers aren't giving you enough bass. Not to shove his foot directly into his mouth, but I begged to differ. Suicide is always senseless, because the suffering that leads to it makes no sense at all – the insanity of the cause assures the illogic of the effect. Only God knows why Lucy had to kill herself; only God knows why her brain waged war against her; only God knows why she suffered, and for whom. I don't and can't and won't, ever. Not until I'm dead, too.

*****

Her official diagnosis was Temporal Lobe Epilepsy, or T.L.E. It was a fickle disease, a changeable disease, a prism of shifting psychiatric and neurological colors. From one angle, it looked like a straightforward seizure disorder: she suffered sudden, neurologically discrete attacks that could be tracked and recorded on an E.E.G. From another, it looked like manic depression: she spun wildly from ecstasy to despair. And from yet another, it looked like psychosis: she hallucinated smells (excrement), sights (moving objects, a rotting leg, surfaces that "breathed"), sounds (voices, sirens).

She had homicidal urges and other violent impulses. She felt bugs crawling up and down her body, biting her everywhere, all the time. She had feelings of déjà vu, jamais vu (the sense of doing something for the first time that's actually been done before), depersonalization (the ripping of mind from brain), dizziness, being trapped in a box, being trapped on another planet, being trapped outside everyone else's reality. She had trouble sleeping. She had trouble talking (word-switching, letter-changing), thinking, judging, remembering, and knowing where she was. She repeated all thoughts several times. She was mad at herself, at well people, at doctors, at lost dreams and useless, jagged fantasies. She felt shame and guilt. She felt alternately possessed by the devil and in the presence of God, who often sat in the room with her during her years of conversion in college. She was hyper-religious, hypersensitive, hypersexual (in urge if not in action), hypergraphic (she wrote constantly, compulsively) and prone to obsessive-compulsive thinking and behavior. She cut herself in the arm to distract from the pain everywhere else.

Nothing helped. At one time or another she'd gulped back two or three dozen kinds of drugs (Zoloft! Xanax! Valium! Elavil! Sinequan! Lithium! Cytomel!

Doxepin! Serax! Valporic Acid! Buspar! Trazodone! Dalmane! Tegretol! Zarontin! Restoril! Clonazepam! Lorazepam! Imipramine! Prozac! Cylert! Haldoperidol! Cogentin! Etcetera! Etcetera! Blah Blah Blah!). Some of these fought seizure disorders. Some fought depression. Some fought anxiety. Some fought insomnia. Some fought psychosis. Some fought the side effects brought on by the drugs fighting seizure disorder, depression, anxiety, insomnia or psychosis. Some (the Cytomel, for instance) fought the long-term organ-function problems brought on by having taken so many prescription medications for so long. But all of them fought Lucy, who was so desperate for a cure that she committed herself to psych hospitals thirteen or fourteen times (I've forgotten which), including half a dozen stays on the nattily manicured campus of Maclean Psychiatric Hospital outside Boston. During a stretch in the Deaconness (in Boston proper) she underwent electro-convulsive therapy, which rocketed her into an artificial high for a while but later failed like everything else. She hoped her doctors would find a locus for her seizures, because that would have given them something specific to cut out. Lucy would have given away half her brain, if she thought it would make her well. She was desperate for a lobotomy.

The problem, despite her years of hospitalizations and drugs and treatments and therapies (shrinks, neuropsychopharmacologists, counselors), was that she never entirely trusted the folks who treated her. Lucy did not believe that they believed that she was as ill as she said she was. Before she was termed a temporal lobe epileptic she was stuck with a sheaf of other labels, including major depressive disorder, manic-depressive disorder, antisocial personality disorder, obsessive-compulsive personality disorder, panic disorder, histrionic disorder, and, that stinking garbage-heap of psychiatric diagnoses, borderline personality disorder. I have to watch it here: I am a stung family member, not a schooled psychologist, and I understand that borderline is a sometimes necessary and accurate diagnosis. I have friends whose lives were plagued by relationships with borderline people. But in Lucy's case, it struck me as nothing more than a tag some lazy doctors applied when they had no freaking idea what to do with her. It meant, more or less, that she was pathologically manipulative and uncooperative and thus had to be treated as pathologically manipulative and uncooperative, regardless of protestations to the contrary (which were, of course, merely manifestations of her pathological manipulativeness and lack of cooperation). Once Lucy was diagnosed as borderline she had a hard time shaking it, simply because everything she said to rebut it was taken as evidence of a borderline personality. So thrums the mill of psychiatry.

Eventually, however, she was diagnosed as a temporal lobe epileptic, and when she was – when she finally held that diagnosis in her sweaty little hand – she felt redeemed. Documentation! Proof! At long last, affirmation from the medical world that she wasn't running from bogeymen, that she wasn't lying, that she was henceforth officially worthy of long-term treatment and vast insurance coverage! The diagnosis was crucial to her hoped-for recovery, because it made tangible what had been, until then, an invisible disease – she had never looked sick. She was too pretty to have a diseased brain; she spoke too well (she was way too articulate about her own deficiencies for them to be taken seriously); she played the piano too well; she was too sweet, too smart, too funny, too educated. The mere fact that a doctor had declared her a textbook temporal lobe epileptic brought her more relief than all the Doxepin she ever swallowed. Once they had a diagnosis, she figured, maybe they could find a cure.

Ha.

*****

Lucy Madeleine Biancolli was born on 17 October, 1960, to a glamorous 37-year-old concert violinist and a 53-year-old classical music critic who looked like a shorter, barrel-chested, cheerfully paesano version of mid-career Cary Grant. Born two weeks late following a long, precarious labor in which her tiny head got stuck, chin up, in the birth canal, Lucy would have died (Mama said) had the obstetrician not seized her temples with forceps and pulled. Out she came, capped with Daddy's thick black hair and possessing a lambent blue regard that came from Mama.

She was Mama's first child -- following one miscarriage -- and Daddy's second. Two decades earlier he had welcomed his first daughter, Margaret, with his first wife, Edith, whom he loved for her generous spirit (she caught his eye at a concert, or was it a lecture, when she gave up her seat to an elderly latecomer) and who later died of heart trouble. Daddy and Mama met in the offices of The New York World-Telegram & The Sun at Barclay and Hudson streets in lower Manhattan, the morning after one of Mama's New York performances. Mama wanted to know why Daddy hadn't reviewed her concert; Daddy snapped back that he "couldn't cover everything," although he dang well tried. In 1958, they were married, taking their vows before a justice of the peace in Queens. Daddy had resisted marriage, just as he had resisted falling in love: Mama caught him off guard with their first kiss, abruptly swiveling her head to catch his chaste cheek-peck full on the mouth.

The two of them were sitting cross-legged on the floor of a Japanese restaurant when Jeanne lobbed the big one at Louis. He replied, "Naaah, don't marry me. I don't have any money. Marry that doctor friend of yours." Naaah, she said, and dragged him off to Queens. They took the subway but were so overwhelmed by the gravity of their decision that they forgot to get off at the Court House and rode all the way to the train yard. Then they rode all the way back. At some point they got off. And got married.

And two years down the road of life and lenitive distractions, Lucy was born.

She was a radiant baby -- pink as a Renaissance cherub, plump with imperfect beauties (a double chin, a crooked smile) that speak of the divine. Daddy told Mama that holding Lucy almost made him believe in God. He wouldn't let it; he shoved it away; yet the revelation stayed with him, settling deep within him like a fine gold dust. Only decades later did a buildup of brilliant yellow ore appear, and by then he weighed it not in ounces but in pounds. So much of it came from Lucy. From the moment she entered the world until her final, exhausted departure, she spread God around her without a blink or a touch of ego. She was unalloyed: bright, clear, and blameless, free from the sullying grot that sticks to the workaday world. The illness that got her was something apart: something alien, something that wasn't her fault. The church of another era might have seen an evil spirit and tried to exorcize it. For all I know, it might have worked.

I don't remember much about Lucy's conversion. I don't remember the details of it the way I do Mama's, which consumed the family, or Daddy's, which occurred on his deathbed while I was more or less literally taking notes. In my memory Lucy grew overnight from stick-limbed heathen child to pious young adult. In my memory she lurched from disbelief to belief with sudden and startling devotion. In my memory she never questioned her budding faith but gave herself up to it entirely, yielding to God's will in a way I hardly grasped. Perhaps that's why I don't remember the details: It seemed foreign to me. The meat of it, too, occurred while Lucy was off at college, so any and all late-night theological musings took place outside my purview. I know she took an Old Testament course that solidified her knowledge of the Bible. I know she took a New Testament course that transformed her knowledge into faith. Beyond that, I know only that the Lucy who returned home on vacations was a Lucy far more transcendent than any I could cope with on a daily basis, having assumed an unearthly goodness that seemed to cast a harsh glance on my own earthly shortcomings. I did not realize at the time that Lucy had, by this point, actually seen God, nor did I realize (as she explained to me later) that the urgency and depth of her conversion were related at least in part to the urgency and depth of her T.L.E. Lucy believed that history is scattered with the divine revelations of temporal lobe epileptics: Joan of Arc, or Saul who became Paul on the road to Damascus. That both met grisly martyr's deaths was a point that escaped me but not Lucy. Never Lucy.

I am not trying to canonize my sister; Lucy had her flaws. But I'm startled, still, by her response to something I once said out of frustration. Angered by Lucy's condition and God's bonehead refusal to cure her, I barked: "Why is God doing this to you! What's the point of it! It's not fair! (duh.) You didn't ask to be a saint!" To which Lucy replied: "I did."

I have to hand it to her: She seemed a bit chagrined. I would say she seemed regretful, only I'm not sure she was; certainly, I'd be regretful for any prayer that plunged me into a state of incurable despair (call me faithless), but then, I'm not Lucy. No, wait, let me check. Yup: still alive. Still a bit of a slowpoke on the road to martyrdom. Sorry.

Lucy became intrigued by sainthood in college, during the first, scarlet flush of her conversion. Her new-found passion for Christ sparked within her the rashest, maddest, most irreversible, insatiable and illogical desire that a human being can harbor: to suffer and die and be a fool for God. It's not part of my nature to ask for pain -- I accept that it will come, no matter my weak machinations to the contrary -- and I will never understand Lucy's holy lust or the prayer that expressed it. I may never forgive her for uttering it. But I accept that Lucy was touched (by God, by illness, by insanity, by death) in a way that I am not, and I accept that this touch brought with it a sort of horrid grace. Suffering makes no sense; loss makes no sense; God makes no sense. God allowed Lucy to suffer. Perhaps God wanted her to suffer -- perhaps she was born to suffer, to carry her crooked light from womb to grave, from toddler waddles through diffident youth to the teetering struggles of adulthood. Looking at photos from her childhood, I scan for hints of her death -- I wonder whether tragedy framed that little face, whether the perfect plump joy in her eyes held some luminous hint of illness. If so, I can't find it: all I see is a darling girl. Perhaps that's all there was.

She was, as toddlers go, remarkable. She walked early, talked early and displayed a prodigious self-awareness from an early age. Mama loved to describe the morning when she hefted Lucy onto the changing table, then turned to answer the telephone. Mother blabbed with unseen friend while the squirt on the table patiently awaited new undergarments. Finally, fed up with the delay, Lucy squeaked in annoyance: "Meanwhile, here I am in wet diapers." Lucy didn't remember that. Mama swore it was true.

When Lucy was four and I was one, we four walked down the hill to the home of a steel-haired retired couple whose sofa was sealed in plastic (*crink*, it said as I sat on it). We shared dinner with them and another guest, a middle-aged man with heart trouble. During the middle of the meal he felt overcome by exhaustion and asked to be excused from the table. The remaining group then fell into talk of Scrabble and politics and the flood of '55, and no one noticed when a black-haired child wandered off into a nearby bedroom. Only when my parents announced it was time to head home did they notice Lucy was gone -- they found her in a chair at the infirm gentleman's bedside, chatting merrily. She had tumbled in, asked if he was sick and then informed him with precocious charity that she would stay and keep him company for a while. He received her visit with grateful amazement. "Who *is* this child?" he asked my parents, and all they could say was: Lucy.

As she grew her generosity grew with her. Riding
the school bus she befriended one outcast after another,
dirt-poor kids who sat in the long back seat and ignored the
childish insults that rained on them from the front. "You're
the only one who talks to me, Lucy," said one such boy,
known for his malodorous clothes and the bag of candy
that he clutched forever in his lap. Even I ignored this
child; even I looked on, thrilled and repulsed, as Lucy
accepted a Tootsie Roll from his stash. So attuned was she
to the pain of all beings (except ants; she loathed ants and
crushed them ruthlessly on sight) that she routinely
liberated grains of rice from Mama's cruel grasp. Decades
later Mama and Lucy laughed about it, this Kitchen Rice
Crusade, but at the time it was a deadly serious
undertaking. She would wait for a piece of rice to fall, then
grab it, refusing to throw her helpless charge into the trash.
One evening, clutching the rescued grain to her chest, she
burst into tears.

It was an excess of conscience, or emotion, or
empathy, this inability to regard anything with detachment.
Much later, during a period when Lucy was struggling
with an addiction to Xanax as well as unremitting
suicidality, she told me that she could no longer process
beauty: She recognized it, but it caused her indescribable
pain. She said this on a boat off the crashing cold coast of
Ullapool, Scotland, where around us rose cliffs of
magnificent and ragged beauty. "Beauty hurts -- it's too
much, I can't take it," she said simply, and I could see the
anguish in her face. Beauty in all of its forms (a painting, a
book, a child, an aria, a tree) gave her no pleasure. Its point
was too sharp, her armor too thin. For beauty to affect us
we need to yield a little bit, we need to feel the prick; our
defenses can't be impenetrable. But listening to her talk, I
was reminded of something a particularly wise English
teacher of mine once said of Sylvia Plath -- that she was a
woman born without skin, for whom the gentlest sensation
caused distress. And although Lucy mercifully survived
that period and later gleaned great joy from beauty, she

never grew insensitive to the gnaws and cricks of life. Nothing mattered little to her.

I always felt, in this regard, that Lucy and I were born with different equipment. I was outfitted for rough weather, while she was not. The soles of my boots were tougher, my wool coat warmer, my gloves more thickly lined. I clunk through my day-to-day world with artless but cheerful resolve, working the odd jobs of human existence: facing this minor setback, ignoring that one, plucking small victories from the ground before they're crushed underfoot. Lucy's course through life was graceful but more precarious, like a sinuous mountain road that promises a thousand-foot plunge to the foolhardy motorist. Every which way she turned, she faced precipitous drops.

Yet she wasn't afraid of heights. Nor did she fear her own death wish. She knew it was there, saw that it threatened her, backed away on her tip-toes and held on tight to keep from slipping -- but she wasn't paralyzed by vertigo. She was, in fact, fantastically cool-headed about the whole incurable-mental-illness ordeal, staring down one fat maw of an abyss with exquisite composure. As an adult she guided me down from the sheer side of Arthur's Seat in Edinburgh, where the two of us had strayed from the path and where I, not she, became petrified by fear. I grabbed at loose soil, peered down the cliff at a dot-sized police car, hyperventilated, panicked, got light-headed, wigged out, broke into tears and froze. "Calm down, Ame," said Lucy, who was accustomed to death's proximity and faced the cliff with astonishing ho-hum ease. "We'll figure this out. We'll get down. I promise." I believed her and followed her to safety: Lucy saved my life.

This same, preternatural calm was apparent even as a child of nine, when she shocked the grownups at a garden party by falling flat on her back, *whoomp*, onto the prickly August grass. The adults assumed it was an accident, but it wasn't. It was one of Lucy's little unexpected experiments: She thought it'd be neat to see what it felt like to fall backward until her head hit the ground. Clearly, an empiricist at heart. But she was driven as well, I think, by a darker motive, by a quiescent desire to not merely approach the precipice but to plunge silently to its floor.

*****

My father knew a man who goosed a friend off the New Jersey Palisades. A thumb in the rump, a jump off the edge, The End. The guy went mad with grief.

Lucy Lucy, Lucy Goosey, Lucy Goosey, I love you. Lucy Goosey, I love you.

Lucy Goosey -- that's what I called her. And oh my God, she goosed herself.

*****

Lucy was in college when she realized something fiendish was going on inside her head. In retrospect, she would recall moments in childhood when she hallucinated or felt a cloud of sadness fog her world – on some obscure level she knew she wasn't supposed to feel that way, she knew such thoughts and images and emotions set her apart from other children. Yet it was years before she realized that grass wasn't supposed to wriggle like tendrils in the morning sun; that the feces she saw and sniffed about her wasn't real; that the disconnectedness that slashed her life from others' was pathological, terrifying, wrong.

And for the most part – certainly by most outsiders' standards – she thrived. All through grade school and grammar school and high school Lucy achieved, in every subject. She wrote beautifully, learned French quickly, grasped subtle concepts with ease and solved math problems with barely a glance at a textbook. She buzzed through homework and studied only occasionally. When she took notes, which she rarely did, she kept them not in neatly ordered notebooks but on random sheets of paper that she often couldn't find when it was time to study for a test. It didn't matter. She loved tests; tests loved her; she aced just about every exam she ever took. In seventh grade her teachers wanted to bump her up a grade, but our parents wouldn't allow it; they didn't want to punish her for being smart. So she stayed where she was, wowing all and getting a reputation as a terrific whiz kid.

At home she was an ambitious young musician. Introduced to the piano at age 8 (long in the tooth, by most standards), she took quickly and passionately to the instrument and before long was devoting hours a day to practice. I remember the day she came home from her first lesson. I asked her to play something for me, expecting to hear something along the lines of Beethoven's Waldstein Sonata, or at least "This Old Man." She said "Sure!," then plopped down at the keyboard and produced a C natural. "IS THAT ALL?" I yelled. She hit it a few more times: It was really a very good C natural, a nice, round middle C that resonated quite breezily around the living room. As a debut performance, it was nothing short of brilliant. But I was dissatisfied. I wanted *more*. I never thought of this before, but it may well be that I was in fact the catalyst for Lucy's professional ambitions: I, the 5-year-old malcontent, her first listener, manager, critic and muse.

At first she played on an old white baby grand that had survived the move from Queens to Connecticut. It was a bristly maiden aunt of an instrument, its keyboard streaked with cracked ivory and splintered wood, its mechanisms squeaky and worn. Lucy had no monopoly on it during her first years of study. Mama played the piano almost as well as she played the violin, and Daddy liked to hammer out his dissonant arrangements of tin pan alley tunes. I took lessons for a few years and quit, fed up with the human pricker bush who was paid to teach me. Lucy stuck with her ("stuck" being the operative word as applied to "pricker") not out of fondness for the woman, who was a good friend of my mother's for no immediately discernible reason, but because she was willing to endure anything to master the piano. Hence she endured Mrs. X, Mrs. X's nippy dachsund, her equally nippy criticisms, and the tone of abject aesthetic horror that Mrs. X assumed when forced to critique a not-fully-prepared piece of music. Mama and I often accompanied Lucy on her piano lessons, mainly to visit with Mrs. X's softspoken husband; Mama would play chess with Mr. X and wander delightedly through his garden. I spent the time dancing around that pissy little dog, who was always aiming to bite somebody.

The backdrop to all of this – the musical score to Lucy's childhood and mine – was the reassuring yet always-vital sound of her practice. Her music was a large part of my life. I awoke on summer mornings to the fluid rattle of scales. I played on the porch to strains of Chopin; I swam as Beethoven splashed in the lake; I flung a ball against the chimney while Brahms brooded inside, bullying Lucy with his dusk-like harmonies. At thirteen, after announcing to Mama and Daddy that she wanted to become a concert pianist, Lucy pushed up her practice time from one or two hours a day to a bruising three or four; most days she was immune to distraction, although I must say I worked hard to supply it. Lucy, lie in the sun with me! Lucy, go swimming with me! Lucy, make asymmetrical useless things out of school paste and egg cartons with me! Go blackberry-picking with me! Watch "Star Trek" with me! (She preferred Chekov to Kirk: betrayal.) Make ornaments with me! Bake gloppy inedible cookie-like objects with me! Play baseball with me!

No, Ame. No, Ame. No, Ame. No, Ame.

I was jealous of her attentions to the piano. Most days I dealt with it, but every now and then the desire to make her life miserable completely overwhelmed me. On one such morning, while my sister was addressing etudes in Deep Fuzzy Artist Mode, I stomped past her on my way upstairs. " Lucy, don't talk to me!'' I yelled.

She ignored me.

"Lucy, DON'T TALK TO ME," I yelled again. This time she stopped playing. She looked at me, nonplused.

"What?" she asked.

"I said, don't talk to me! Just don't talk to me! I don't want you to talk to me!"

"I'm not talking to you," she said.

"Don't talk to me!"

She shrugged -- "Okay, so I won't talk to you" – and went back to them etudes.

"MO-OM! LUCY WON'T TALK TO ME!!!!"

Why I did this, I'm not sure. The payoff was slim and the consequences were immediate – Mother. Was. Not. Happy. – but I think I gleaned some small satisfaction out of spotting incredulity in Lucy's rarely-incredulous face. She was one of the least-flappable people I've ever known. It's what made her so gullible; she could believe anything. "Lucy, did you know that Scandinavians can't spit?" her freshman roommate once asked, and Lucy responded: "Really? Wow!" To a woman who had watched inanimate objects materialize, dematerialize and wiggle like millipedes, nothing seemed incredible.

*****

Every now and then, Lucy stopped playing. She took breaks to pee and eat, and occasionally sleep. Once in a while she was known to pause for Monopoly games at the Adams' house down by the water; she had a stupefying crush on their oldest son and was once caught holding hands with him under a blanket (shhh!) while the bunch of us watched rods of lightning slash across the lake. She broke for figure-skating broadcasts. And movies, sometimes. And school. But never was Lucy more at home than at the piano -- she belonged there. I had no business pulling her from it, for it was there that she became a confident, centered, complete human being. I have so many photographs of her sitting at that Mason & Hamlin,

attacking some recalcitrant chord – her lips pursed, her
wiry hair recoiling from every downbeat, her small, strong
back proudly upright. All of her illness fell away when she
played; all of her insecurity and hesitancy in this prolix
world suddenly peeled and scattered, revealing the hard
core of a performer's ego. Those who knew her only
through her sickness (doctors, fellow psych patients,
friends who'd met her in the last years of her life) were
stunned by her ability at the piano, by her ferocious
presence, her belief in herself, her focus -- little mousy
Lucy had the heart of a jaguar.

I wonder whether Lucy would have died had her
illness not forced her to give up performing. I wonder
whether the piano kept her alive. In one sense, I'm sure it
did – it gave shape to her young life and propelled her
along a strictly delineated path. At Wykeham Rise, the
small, warm, girls' arts school (now long dead) where my
mother taught music, Lucy was regarded as one of the
brightest lights in the pre-professional music program; all
assumed, Lucy included, that she would move on to a
prominent conservatory and thereafter embark on a career
as a concertizing soloist. Before her sixteenth birthday
nothing happened to dissuade us, or her. But mid-way
through her junior year at Wykeham, she took a crushing
blow: Her beloved teacher, a fiery Australian pianist
named Bruce Hungerford, was killed by a drunk driver
while returning home from a concert with his niece and her
husband. After Mama got the call from Bruce's sister, she
trekked up the steep path to Wykeham's music building
and found Lucy practicing at a Steinway on the first floor.
Mama gave her the news, and Lucy wailed – wordlessly,
uncontrollably. Until that moment, Mama later told me,
she had never understood the word "keen."

Lucy was shattered by Bruce's death. At the time I
didn't understand or even perceive it, but this loss was the
single defining trauma of her high school years. It was the
first time, after the deaths of Mama's parents, that she'd
lost a loved one – the first occasion when death actually

reached out its fist and smacked her. We thought we knew all about death; we'd seen it lurking around the house often enough, what with Mama's perpetual hospitalizations (pneumonia, hypertension, organ failure) and Daddy's suicide attempt-cum-coma. We always figured we'd be orphaned some day. The great, miraculous joke of our childhoods was that despite all of the hours we spent anticipating death's arrival -- thinking about it, gawking at it, searching for it in the faces of our sick and creaky parents -- Mama and Daddy didn't die. They survived into our adulthoods. Bruce's death blindsided Lucy because she'd been caught staring in the other direction; it came from an angle she didn't expect.

Nevertheless, she kept at the piano. She found a new teacher: two, actually, one right after the other, neither of which worked out. Both were compassionate and attentive instructors, and both came highly recommended. But they weren't Bruce. Lucy worshiped Bruce; Mama said she was in love with him. Perhaps she was – he was equal parts nonconformity and charisma, much like our own father. I occasionally went along on lesson days, sitting in Bruce's agreeably cramped apartment, accepting the Malomar and glass of cider that our host inevitably proffered. He pulled up a chair and watched while I ate it; I wasn't allowed to refuse. Neither was Lucy. She followed his instructions laboriously and without question (she started off each morning with a tone-developing exercise that involved endless, and I mean endless, repetition of one note), always believing that he would lead her toward a deeper and more incisive musicianship. Whether he did, I don't know – but I do know that Lucy obtained a profundity and precision during Bruce's tenure that she hadn't displayed before. I do know that he lit a fire under her, a passion not simply for playing but for performing – a craving for the stage – and gave her hope that she could and would turn professional. Who knows what might have happened to Lucy's career had Bruce not died. Who knows what might have happened to her life.

In her senior year she applied to music conservatories. Juilliard rejected her. Curtis rejected her. Juilliard she didn't particularly care about (Mama had a long-standing prejudice against the place), but her failure to get into Curtis devastated her. For weeks she awaited word. Every afternoon she walked down the hill to the mailbox and trudged back empty-handed. Mama had taken to phoning the post office early in the morning, so unbearable was the vigil. Finally, one day, Mama got word that a letter from Curtis had arrived, and she bumped to the post office in her pea-green Rabbit. Then she bumped right back. Lucy never forgave Mama for opening the letter en route. She never forgave her for the dampness on Mama's cheeks, or the look of quivering pity that came through the door. She didn't yell, or cry, or lash out at Mama for taking a hurtful liberty. She just went upstairs and lay in her bed, one hand idly stroking her eyebrows as she studied the ceiling and erased her thoughts. She was good at burying anger.

The result of all this was Lucy's decision to enroll at Harvard. Strange as it sounds, Harvard had been Lucy's dead-last choice – she applied mainly because she'd scored almost 1,600 on her SATs and didn't know quite what to do with them. Not applying to Harvard would have seemed an appalling waste; she didn't even bother sending off applications to other, lesser colleges. Brilliant as she was, a tested genius who whiffed through every homework assignment that crossed her path, she had no gripping ambition beyond the desire to make music. That was enough: she burned for the piano, for the career she had envisioned and pursued since childhood. All else was secondary. And her resigned decision to go to Harvard, in the context of her young, bustling ambition, was in many ways a source of immense disappointment.

It was there, in her first two years of college, that Lucy's illness first began to affect her music-making and, ultimately, her life. She continued playing – she continued taking lessons, this time with a fierce Hungarian taskmaster, and she kept one foot on the stage in small and large recitals. Her freshman year was difficult in many ways (communal-living woes; huge-and-impersonal-university woes; woes of the heart), but she did manage to stay true to her one lasting swain, music. Not until her sophomore year at Harvard did the cord twining her to the piano begin to fray.

Years after the fact she told me she'd quit because she'd found it impossible to learn new music – that the T.L.E. barred her from concentrating and so bollixed her mental processes that she could no longer focus on the short term (the piece at hand) or the long term (her career). Certainly this period accompanied her first real flirt with Catholicism, a platonic dalliance that grew into a convert's dizzy love. Just as certainly, she was distracted from her music by her preoccupation and eventual affair with a fellow pianist, a former student of Bruce's with wooden good looks and a cool disposition. To me he seemed haughty; to me he seemed remote and unappreciative of my sister; and so I loathed him. She knew I loathed him, he knew I loathed him, everyone knew I loathed him. (Mama loathed him, too: "His eyes are too close together! Tch!") Whether he deserved to be loathed is unclear to me now, viewing the past from the fire tower of my middle years, but back then I regarded it as not simply my right but my sacred duty. I was Lucy's little sister; it was my job to hate his guts.

Lucy's affair with this man was a source of constant anguish, but I can hardly blame him for her abandonment of the piano. Nor can I blame him for the troubles that followed: her final years at Harvard (where she converted, fought and endured, struck by melancholy but filled with the crazy new light of faith), her post-college meandering from Italy (where she studied to be a Montessori teacher, of all things, a goal pursued for multifarious complicated reasons that boiled down to not knowing what the hell else to do) to Connecticut (where she taught Montessori) to Minnesota (where she taught music) to Connecticut again (where she lived at home and worked as a typesetter for a weekly newspaper) to Cambridge (where she earned scandalously little slaving away for an environmental health publication).

In Cambridge she was finally, irreversibly halted by her illness. It forced her to go on disability and fixed her in the Boston area. Most of her doctors were there; most of her friends were there; and after a while I was, too. Three years before Lucy died I moved in with her and a third roommate, in the first-floor apartment of a triple-decker clapboard house in Somerville, a northwestern suburb of Boston. I liked living there with her, although the madness of it terrified me: I knew she had a fatal illness. I knew she would die some day. I knew that not an hour passed when Lucy didn't entertain killing herself. She and I discussed the likelihood of her suicide many times. It was the reason I moved in. Not to save her, mind you – not to take care of her, keep an eye her, seize sharp implements and switch her knives for spoons – but just to be with her. I was there to hug her, to watch bloody thrillers on TV with her and eat long tubes of Toblerone while talking about men and laughing. Sometimes I'd scratch my armpits like a chimp and OOH-OOH-AHH-AHH around the apartment, just to cheer her up. ("Do the gorilla, Ame!") "Lucy, promise me you won't kill yourself," I'd say, knowing it was a stupid thing to ask, knowing she couldn't agree. She'd look at me sadly, her face softening with love and pity. "I'll try, Ame." So often she told me that I and Mama and Daddy were the reasons she fought the urge. Killing herself was the easy part; it was only the thought of hurting us that stayed her hand.

She did make one previous, serious attempt. It occurred in early 1990 and followed one of her least-successful hospitalizations – one of those many occasions when she went in sick and, presto-change-o!, came out sicker. In the weeks leading up to the attempt she was in constant tears. She spoke hours at a stretch on the telephone and carefully plotted each day so that she would, at no point, have the opportunity to commit suicide. Solitude was the devil. So raw was her despair that Mama eventually drove up from Connecticut to be with her, hearing imminent death in her sobs. Daddy had no idea what was going on, but Mama didn't want to leave him at home, so they took a hotel room in North Cambridge and Lucy collapsed there.

That afternoon they all took naps. Daddy slept in one twin bed, Mama and Lucy in the other. Lucy awoke first. She padded over to her purse and pulled out an assortment of bottles. She opened them, poured them, swallowed. She waited. She looked at Mama; she looked at Daddy. Then, in one sudden, lucid moment, she realized what she'd done and roused Mama, saying what had to be said in a groggy rush of words (mamamama IjusttookpillsmamalistenwakeupIjustdiditpleaselistenmama listenwakeupIjusttookpills) before crashing once more on the bed. Mama phoned the hospital. Right then I arrived, thinking we were all going off to supper (meet us at 5 at the hotel room, 'kay?) but knowing in a half-second of horrified comprehension that Lucy had finally done it. "Don't be mad at me," she said, and Mama said, "We have to get her downstairs before she falls unconscious," and I said, "Lucy," and she said again, "Don't be mad at me," and I said, "I'm not." And I wasn't. Even when I visited her in the hospital that night, even when I saw her in a coma wrapped in tubes and sucking bottled air, even when I knew she had done something wretched, even when I realized: Jesus Christ! My father did this, too! I saw my father this way, too! -- even then, I wasn't mad at her. I didn't want to be mad at her; anger would have taken up too much space in my brain. I had other things to worry about.

She was in a coma for three days. Mama stayed by her side while I drove Daddy home to Connecticut and looked after him, cooking up reassuring half-truths (Lucy Will Be Fine, Oh Yes) and plentiful frozen food. After a while Mama came home, and I went back to

Massachusetts, and Lucy came back to our flat in
Somerville. She seemed shaky, regretful; we both knew
that if she ever pulled the same stunt again, there'd be no
homecoming afterwards. Suicide had always been a
possibility, but her first attempt pushed it out of the future
and into the toxic present. It turned real.

*****

Lucy was always smarter than I was. She was
always more devout. She was nicer, kinder, cleaner,
funnier, more graceful (she excelled at ballet; I'm pigeon-
toed), a better musician, a lovelier singer, a more gifted
student, a more brilliant test-taker, a more profound poet, a
more natural writer and a more open and purer child of
God than I am or ever will be. By comparison I am dull-
witted, tin-eared, toad-voiced, mud-covered, thick-skulled,
left-footed, Godless and nasty. There are a couple things I
do well that Lucy never mastered: soccer, softball, athletic
pursuits in general. I'm a better driver than she was (wow).
In high school I took lots of ceramics courses that she
never attempted, so, hey, she never made a pinch pot.
Growing up in Lucy's shadow was hard until I figured out
that I didn't have to be her: I could juggle my soccer ball
and get my As and Bs (not A-pluses – not like Lucy) and
go on to a neat liberal arts college where no one knew that
Lucy existed, where no one knew that I was the stupider of
the two. Imagine my amazement when I realized I was
bright. And imagine my amazement when I, not Lucy, not
the Great She-Woman of Thundering Academic Success,
went on to a rewarding career.
    Lucy was gifted at everything but life. I mastered
that with a gusto she couldn't – as skilled she was at
everything else, she lacked the ability to live. I cringe,
now, when people draw too much attention to early
childhood achievement, as though intellectual and
academic success inevitably foretell future happiness. I'll
tell you a secret: It doesn't. The two smartest people I've

ever known were also bent on killing themselves. Daddy tried once. Lucy tried twice, second time lucky. So, no, I don't want my kids to make themselves miserable getting into Harvard -- if they get there, great, but only if it brings them peace. I don't want them to earn their doctorates in chaos theory at age fifteen. I'm glad they're smart and interested in the world, but in the end I just want them to live -- breathe in, breathe out, nice rosy complexions, their hearts sloshing blood, squish-squish, squish-squish, squish-squish, until they reach their 80s and die in their sleep. I don't desire for them anything beyond health and long life and contentment. The rest is moot. I'd rather my little ones grow up average and happy than geniuses puking bile.

*****

Lucy. Luce. Lucinolde, I called her. I was Aminolde. I also called her JoAnn Fish, although I'm not sure why; maybe her old friend Royce thought it up when they were teenagers. Lucy accepted, liked and used it, often signing notes alongside a scribbled caricature of a plump bespectacled guppy with frizzy black hair and a foolish grin. I once made (and now own, since Mama's death) a thick earthenware bowl that bore JoAnn's name and visage on the side. For years Mama kept it as a candle holder, later as a receptacle for strange asymmetrical objects like chipped buttons and small bent pins and rusty thumbtacks and other orphaned doodads, eventually relegating the vessel to Amy's Dead-Ceramics Cemetery located on the uppermost living room shelf (look! check out that elephant-shaped cookie jar!). I admired its similar location in our own home until my husband started using it as a water dish for the rabbit. So JoAnn Fish lives on.

Lucy was a great goof, an inspired talker, a lover of music and art and movies and non sequiturs both verbal and visual. Among the paintings she most admired were those of Magritte, whose surreal skyscapes and floating bodies mirrored her own oblique and tenuous residency on earth. She had a screwball sense of humor, a startling appreciation for the absurd and no fear of indulging either. In the kitchen with Daddy and a camera one morning, Lucy grabbed a banana and stuck it between two buttons on his blue corduroy shirt. She grabbed a second banana and stuck it down his open neck. She grabbed a third and stuck it in his breast pocket. She grabbed a fourth and stuck it in his -- I'm not sure where, exactly. From the looks of things the fruit either hung from a piece of fishline or hovered, thanks to some unseen levitating-vegetable power, over his left ribcage. She grabbed Mama's knit turquoise cap and stuck it on his head. She grabbed an apple and stuck it on the cap. Then she grabbed the camera and stuck it in his face, telling him to mug as the spirit moved him. The spirit moved him to mug wholeheartedly, his eyes popped with outrage, his wide-open mouth a big wet ring. *Snap.* (Look closely: That's yesterday's lunch, or maybe the day before the day before yesterday's lunch, balancing on jar-tops to the right.)

We liked to play with tape recorders, she and I: the Adams kids would trot up the hill to our house and we would spend hours hunched over a microphone, recording horror tales, fake news broadcasts and spoof radio commercials sporting creatively generated sound effects. ("This is the sound of Softies Underwear, floating gently down the staircase" -- cue cast-iron pans.) Not long ago I ran across one of these old tapes, barely audible, shot through with pounding white noise. Amid the hiss can be found the following exchange:

Lucy (assuming high-pitched, agonizingly nasal voice):
    You're weeeeeeeeeeeeird.
Me (assuming lower-pitched, agonizingly nasal voice):
    Well, you're weeeeeeeeeeeeeirder.
Lucy: Well, you're weeeeeeeeeeeeeirder.
Me: You're even weeeeeeeeeeeeirder.
Lucy: No, you're weeeeeeeeeeeeeirder.

Me: No, you're weeeeeeeeeeeeeeirder.
Lucy: You're weird, not me.
Me: You're weird.
Lucy: You're weird.
Me: You're weird.
> (Pause; fumbling in background; vague words about pizza. Then:)

Me: Snob!
Lucy: Snot!
Me: Imbecile!
Lucy: Dorman!
Me: Weirdo!
Lucy: STRANGE PERSON!!!

And then no more -- that's it. "Dorman," incidentally, is shorthand for "Normal person who says 'duh,' " and don't ask me where it came from. I think it's something Lucy cooked up with Kathy Adams. "STRANGE PERSON" -- always rendered in capital letters -- was actually a term of endearment, and was usually (though not in this case) pronounced by splitting the first word into two elongated syllables: STRRR-ANGE PERSON.

Lucy loved being an oddball; she had a genius for it, a genius streaked with mischief. Once, in college, she was invited to a holiday gathering by someone who had rubbed her the wrong way, possibly a sheath-dressed social-X-ray-in-training who brazenly snoot-nosed the purple-crepe spaghetti-strap gown Lucy had worn to a chichi undergraduate fete. I guess everyone else was in taupe. Saintly Lucy exacted her revenge (with Royce, her forever conspirator) by whipping up cookie dough spiced with marjoram, mace, pepper, onion powder and oregano, then forming it into turd-shaped blobs. She and Royce brought the finished product to the party, slipped it furtively onto the buffet table and retreated into the shadows, where they spent the rest of the affair watching guests spit out offending chunks of half-chewed cookie.

Hints of a great criminal mastermind were evident in childhood. Chief among the early indicators was a plan that involved Lucy (6) and me (3) rising in the middle of the night and walking unchaperoned into town. The idea, as I understood it, was to go shopping with a stash of Monopoly money. At no point did it occur to us that the stores might be closed at 2 a.m., or that the shop owners might not accept play money printed in pastel hues, or that one of them might telephone our parents the moment Lucy and I wandered in, clad in furry-toed pajamas. Nor did it occur to us that Lucy might make so much noise while rousing me (I refused to get up) that she would wake the household and incur the wrath of Mama.

She was not a shrinking violet -- a violet, to be sure, but a violet with teeth. Most chronically sick people aren't, for no more complicated reason than they can't afford to be. Despite her child-like generosity, Lucy had no fondness for boors or selfish twits and could pull off a fair imitation of a rude rejoinder, if the situation demanded it. During that spell in Minnesota, where she spent a fraught, frozen year teaching piano and making ends meet at a greasy spoon called the Lemon Drop (aren't they all?), she rebuffed a crabbish patron who complained about a hair in her soup by snapping, "Well! Hairs have a way of falling out!'' She felt powerfully about politics and despised Bill Clinton – this was *before* he got elected – with lavish hyperbole. I remember her last remarks about him, in March 1992: "I HATE Bill Clinton. I HATE everything about him. I HATE his face. I HATE his body. I HATE his hair. I HATE HIM.'' (Michael Dukakis, on the other hand, she admired, forget the loss in '88. And she adored Paul Tsongas.)

She loved chocolate. She loved Mikhail Baryshnikov. She loved "The Pink Panther'' movies. She loved Camus. She loved Bach songs – she loved to sing them (in a radiant soprano), she loved to hear them, she loved the fact that they existed. She loved cats. She loved sandals. She loved raisin bread. She loved dippy snappy

pop songs. She loved to dance. She loved tea; she
expressed this love by filling her mug to surface-tension
point and setting it at the very very very very edge of a
table, preferably a really wobbly table, and then yelling
"DON'T TOUCH THE TABLE" at anyone in touching
distance. She loved ice cream. She loved creamed herring.
She loved the French language. She loved "Chariots of
Fire." She loved the Ode to Joy. She loved the Sonata for
Violin and Piano by César Franck, which she performed
with Mama (I turned pages). She loved to laugh and make
other people laugh and make bizarre faces and channel
funny voices through her nose. She loved to throw her
springy black mass of hair over her face and then put on
her glasses over it. She loved stuffed animals. She loved
little pretty things. She loved earrings. She loved beads.
She loved large, comfy sweatshirts with whimsical designs
– her favorite, which she often wore when hospitalized,
featured a bowl of smiling fruit. She loved her family. She
loved life.

To wit: the irony of suicide. Those who commit it
love life more than the rest of us; they battle the urge to die
daily, hourly, second-to-second. They know what a
precious thing it is to live.

Lucy did what she needed to do to get attention (to
get care; to get going; to get heard), regardless of public
befuddlement or opprobrium. One summer afternoon, in
the grip of unbearable horniness -- a side-effect of her
illness or her meds -- Lucy threw herself around the trunk
of a small tree along the banks of the Charles River and
refused to let go. It was something to hold. On a similar
outing she became overcome by the sun and, ignoring the
horrified cries of onlookers, plunged clothed but shoeless
into the dingy Boston waters. Around the same time she
caused a stir in a hip Cambridge coffee house notorious for
lax service. After waiting forty-five minutes for someone
to take her order, she stood in front of her chair. Then she
stood on her chair. When that failed to work, she stood on
the table, after which a waiter miraculously appeared. Lucy

climbed down and ordered, acting as though nothing out of the ordinary had just occurred. In her view, any strategy that obtained for her any single thing or combination of things required for her bodily or spiritual equilibrium (be it an anti-convulsant or a decaf cappuccino) was a perfectly reasonable and viable modus operandi. She really didn't care what people thought.

For instance: The cone-shaped mass of gauze that she wore around her head for a day or two while taking an ambulatory EEG at Maclean. It was quite an impressive headdress -- terrifying in its size, comical in its inevitable pop analogy to Jane Curtin in Full Conehead on" Saturday Night Live." I signed her out of Maclean one night and took her down the hill to a Greek diner, where several alert patrons paused, mid-meatloaf, to stare gape-mouthed (and -eyed and -nostriled) at Lucy's pointy white chapeau. "What's that on your head?" our waitress asked. Lucy replied, beautifully deadpan, "An iron lung." The waitress said "Oh." That's all she could manage: "Oh."

It may be that Lucy's illness cured her of petty worries, or it may be that she never had any to begin with; even as a teenager, she certainly wasn't one to fret over the opinion of peers. By the time she hit her late twenties she'd become a fierce individualist, a woman so preoccupied with the top priority (not dying) that all small concerns faded to gray. For someone so stymied by neurological dysfunction and low self-esteem, she was remarkably stubborn about getting her own way. She pushed to get treatment, pushed to get insurance coverage, pushed to get doctor's appointments, pushed to get heard. Her enormous eyes, round as quarters and always on the verge of laughter or tears, belied the coil of strength within her, the obstinate refusal to back down until she'd made her point. For to back down, would have meant to die. From disability came empowerment – like the husky biceps on a man in a wheelchair, it was born of necessity.

*****

I loved her. I had to love her -- it's all I could do. Her illness simplified matters: I couldn't waste time getting offended or annoyed. Nothing breaks my heart, these days, more than stories of adult siblings who don't talk to each other, who allow grudges to widen into canyons of silence. Lucy and I *talked*. Not just about guys and snubs and jobs and joys, but about everything, every wee thing in every corner of our lives, every fear, every hope, every hidden truth. We talked about her suicidality. We talked about how I would cope (or not) if she died; I told her how much I would miss her, how it would kill me if she killed herself. One of my most unexpected urges in the weeks following her death was the desire to reassure her – to say, Hey, guess what, Luce, I'm all right. I said it out loud: Lucy, I'm okay. It didn't kill me. You didn't kill me. I'm really okay.

I talk to the dead. To Lucy, to Mama, to Daddy. We talked so much while they were living – even Daddy, though senility and deafness meant he understood less and less as the years wore on – that to shut down communications now, just because I'm living and they're not, would seem an unbearable loss. Old habits die hard, and so do relationships. They're still my family. They're still a part of my life, and I am, I think, still a part of theirs. After I got married (a mere eight months before everyone started dying), Lucy's doctor could hardly wait until I had children. "Little Amys," he called them -- a brood of loved ones to connect Lucy to the world. Though Lucy never met her Little Amys, I believe she loves them, believe she holds them to her, believe she keeps an eye on them at times when I cannot. I dreamed, once, of Lucy cradling Madeleine in her arms. Sometimes I ask her to pray for them. Sometimes I ask her to pray for me. Always, I pray for her.

*****

Lucy was the strongest person I've ever known. Yet I'm the who's still kicking, still clipping my nails and licking peanut butter off of spoons and picking the lint from sweaters. Lucy's done with all that; she's done with lint. When you die at thirty-one there are lots of household chores you leave behind. I didn't die at thirty-one. And now, to my own amazement, I'm older than my older sister; turning thirty-two was surreal. Having lived the first twenty-eight years of my life trailing Lucy by three wide years, I feel peculiar in the lead, pressing past birthdays that my sister never celebrated, marveling at the whitish spider legs that crawl across my face. Lucy didn't live long enough to get a wrinkle. She didn't live long enough to worry about dying her gray, because she didn't have any gray to dye. She didn't live long enough to get married, give birth, buy a house, bury her parents, worry about school districts and watch as her kid sister grew up to do the same. She didn't live long enough to feel that life, which had for so long been so savagely difficult, might someday prove worth living. She resisted suicide each day because she valued existence, because she wanted to *want* to live, because she believed that life truly ought to prevail over death and that God, in creating her, must have had some glorious but hazy reason for putting her here. No one I know desired more than Lucy to keep her feet on terra firma. She fought off death with humor and fortitude. Death nabbed her anyway, leaving me to age in her youthful absence. Her clock stopped first when she died. It stops again each time I regard her face in a photo, or regard my own instead. I change. She does not.

Thinking of Lucy, I wonder whether there's time in heaven. It's a pointless question – I'd just as well ask whether there's air conditioning in heaven, or phone solicitors, or Pizza Huts. In other words, probably not. But the fact of my living, the fact of her dying (always, continually, now as then as ever), and the fact that I cannot imagine existence without activity, mean that my belief in an afterworld demands some notion of linear and spatial movement. Dead Lucy moves through the heaven of my imagination as Live Lucy moved on earth. Motion implies duration; duration is time accrued. Therefore, I conclude, the handsome and spacious Kitchen in the Sky obeys the tick tick tick of an egg timer. *Ding.* Is it time to pull out the brownies? Don't let them turn into hockey pucks!

Are there indeed brownies in heaven? Are there hockey pucks? Is there music? magnetism? mass transit? water? Are there public spaces? private lives? Do people bump into each other in the streets? Are there streets? Do they study in libraries? Are there libraries? If there's art, what does it reflect, if not life? Can art reflect eternity? Can art reflect God? But if human beings are in God's image, does that mean we are works of art? Does heaven hold answers for everything? When I die, will I meet Lucy and Mama and Daddy? Will we speak without voices? Will we know without seeing? Will I kiss them? Will we hug?

After Lucy died, a friend told me, "For the rest of your life, you'll have one foot in heaven." At the time I didn't know what she meant. Now I do. She meant that I, in losing my beloved sister, would forever feel the next world tugging. It would always pull, pull, tilting my head in its vague direction, yanking at the folds of my skirt while I bustle about the errands of my life. I am here; my husband and children are here; my job and joys and friends are here. Yet Lucy -- now Mama, now Daddy -- are there. They will always be there. So There is what I dream about. There is where my mind rests when it wanders. There is where my childhood resides, hardened like clay in the deaths of those who loved me.

4

Candy Man

It was seven weeks since my sister died when my father started talking to her.

He was 85 and in a hospital bed, with a failing heart, a broken hip and pneumonia. A week earlier he had fallen from his bed and had a heart attack. Once renowned for his energy and intellect, he was now a wisp of a man taking erratic gulps of oxygen through a mask in intensive care. I stood at his side and stared at him, wondering whether and when he would die.

He did not know that Lucy had died before him. Mama and I hadn't told him; he was too old, we reasoned, and too confused. Alzheimer's or strokes or brain damage or some other senile dementia had stolen his short-term memory and rendered him unable to recall anything, any person or occurrence, that was not fixed securely in his past. If he learned of Lucy's death he would grieve, then forget, then grieve anew the next time he heard of it. Or so we feared.

Thus Lucy was on my mind, but not my lips, as I held Daddy's hand one warm springtime evening, stroking his brow and telling him I loved him at a volume that, I hoped, would penetrate his deafness. He was awake but not attentive; his wet brown eyes were open wide, focused on the ceiling. Mama was chatting with a nurse outside his room.

Suddenly, he demanded: "Who is that?"

I assumed he was talking to me. It's Amy, I told him. I'm your daughter. I love you.

"Who?"

I repeated myself. Confused, he mumbled something incomprehensible, then asked: "Sister? Whose sister?"

No, I said. I'm Amy. Your daughter.

"Sister? A sister died? Whose sister died?"

I stopped, struck dumb. I looked at Daddy, his eyes trained intently on the ceiling. He mumbled something else I could not fathom, then shut his eyes and fell asleep. When Mama returned I told her what had passed. Her mouth dropped open. Lucy, she said. Lucy, I agreed. We held hands across my father's midriff and stood, silent, as he shook from a dream or a stab of pain.

He said other things that evening. He spoke of lights – "Is that sunshine?" and "Isn't that bright light beautiful?" – and asked repeatedly about the identity of someone or something in the room. The next morning he turned to me and announced, with astonishing matter-of-factness, that he had "experienced a fantastic expansion of love." The expression on his face was clear and peaceful. He spoken of heaven, and Jesus, and God, and the shaft of light nearby. "Is that bright light relevant?" he asked. "Will that bright light fall on us?" A day later he saw Lucy standing at my mother's shoulder.

Daddy, as I've said, was not a religious man – he

was zealous about many things, but God was not one of them. He was devout only in his atheism. He had lost his faith at 19, when his best friend shot himself in the head, and he believed from then on only in the essential goodness of humanity and the social promise of Marxism. He wavered little in his later years, crinkling his nose with distaste at the mention of God or religion. That his wife and two younger daughters converted to Catholicism perplexed him, to be sure, but for our part we didn't bother him too much with evangelical pokes and proddings. Occasionally we'd ask him to join us at Mass, but he always refused. He was a good person, kind, intensely moral and an avowed practitioner of clean living; he was also stubborn. If he found religion, he'd find it in his – and God's – own time.

Perhaps he found it in intensive care. I suspect he did – I believe he did – but for months afterward I hesitated telling people at the risk of sounding crazed, or wishful, or both. What could I say? "My dead sister soothed my Dad in his hospital bed. I heard him speak to her." Right. In an age of science and skepticism, it is difficult, sometimes, to confess publicly to a belief in the supernatural. And yet what happened in that room was surely above and beyond the natural. Or maybe it was entirely natural; maybe, as the priests and rabbis tell us, what Mama and I witnessed was more real than earth.

I hope so. It was hard seeing Daddy wither in bed; it had been hard watching the slow decline that led him there. Over a span of fifteen years he had turned from a man of strapping health and fierce erudition to a sweet, perilously frail old gentleman with a head of thick white hair and no real memory. He knew Mama, he knew Lucy and he knew me, although he frequently couldn't distinguish one of us from the others. He knew, too, that Lucy had been sick for several years, but the complexity of her illness was always beyond his grasp. So was the incurable despair that took her life. "And Lucy? How is Lucy?" he'd often ask, and we'd answer: Sick. He would blink, rub his thumb distractedly against his forefinger, and turn to the crossword puzzle that never left his side. Ten minutes later, he'd ask again: And how is Lucy?

Daddy and Lucy had always had a special friendship. She was the first child born to his second marriage, and she inherited many of his gifts: his whiplash intelligence, his passion for music, his love of conversation. Both were inspired windbags. As a toddler Lucy would lie on the couch with him and the two would gab, loudly and delightedly. Years later, Daddy would sit in the living room while Lucy practiced for hours on end at the Mason & Hamlin. Shod in heavy-soled boots, he'd galumph up behind her and listen, transfixed. "Brava!" he'd yell in her ear, interrupting her practice. "Beautiful! Bravissima!"

It made sense, then, that Lucy was on hand to welcome Daddy to the other side. It made sense that she joined me and Mama at his bed to comfort him. And it made sense, somehow, that despite her death, despite the wall between this world and the next one, our relationship with Lucy hadn't changed at all. She was still our daughter, our sister, our friend. She spoke to my father, and he, not knowing she had died, heard her words and responded.

Almost a month after Daddy first entered the hospital, I noticed once again that he was staring at the ceiling. I asked him what he saw. "That bright light is very near," he said, then paused. His brow wrinkled with worry. Clearly and urgently, in a voice more powerful than any he had used in weeks, he pleaded with the ceiling – was it Lucy? – "Come now! Come now! Come now! Come now!"

Five days later, she did.

*****

I'll say it up front: My father was a strange man. He was a great man. He was impossible to understand,

driven by an indecipherable undercurrent of insecurity and
fear. He was full of paradoxes -- a loving man with a
volcanic temper, a good man plagued by self-hatred, a
brilliant man never quite convinced of his own
accomplishments. He was crazy -- Daddy, I love you, but
you were *crrrrrrazy* -- yet at the same time more spookily
intuitive than anyone in my life. In describing him to
friends I'd say, "He's old," or "He's senile," or "He's kind of
unusual," or "He worries a lot," or "He was a music critic,"
or "He likes languages," or "He's an utterly charming
wacko who'll forget your name two minutes after he's
learned it but will embrace you with the warmth of an old
friend," but nothing I said ever captured him, not
completely. He resisted definition. It seemed to me that
other people's fathers could be rendered in a sentence or
two of neatly-articulated specifics (A Lawyer Who Makes
His Own Wine. An Engineer Who Likes To Go Sailing. A
Teacher Who Carves With a Chain Saw.), while mine
required twelve pages of footnotes. He became, for an
uncomfortable period in my very young adulthood, the
elephant in the bedroom (or the wife in the attic) that I
didn't want to talk about -- my secret weirdo Daddy. Good
friends knew about him. Better friends met him. The best
of all (God bless you, Pam Bond) shared in my blackest
fits of laughter.

He was so complicated, so simple, so infuriating,
so true: The bibliophilic music critic who played by ear.
By ear! And went deaf, or close to it, close enough to wear
hearing aids that he cranked up till they whined like a
siren. Phone conversations were a chore, mainly because
he could rarely find a compromise volume that allowed
him to a) hear but b) not send waves of feedback cascading
into the telephone. "DADDY, TURN UP YOUR
HEARING AIDS! *TURN - THEM - UPPPPP!!!*" I yelled,
infamously, I should add, from a phone booth in the all-
night reading room of the Hamilton College library. The
all-night readers didn't know what they were in for. (Pam
was there; see: "God bless you. . . ," above.) He turned

them up, all right, but he turned them too far up, and then it was a job getting him to turn them down again. But not too far down. But wasn't I glad I phoned? LOVE YOU, DADDY! BYE-EEEE!

No, no, honest -- I loved Daddy deeply, really I did. It just took me a while to get over my agonizing embarrassment at having such old and/or sick and/or staggeringly quirky parents. "Someday you'll stop caring what people think of you," Mama said, and if I remember correctly she was hoisting an empty teapot over her head to flag the waiter's attention in a Chinese restaurant while she said it (see: Lucy, "hip Cambridge coffee shop," above). She was right, of course, but then I was hardly in a position to appreciate it: I was a teenager. It was a perilous time to be my parent. "You guys are OBSOLETE," I hurled at them one day (*j'accuse!*), trying out a new word, and the insult stung them enough that my mother referred it for years. I think it cut too close to home; they were always getting mistaken for my grandparents, especially Daddy. I'm not sure how this affected him, or if it did. I never thought to ask him how he felt. I never thought to ask him lots of things. I suppose, when you get right down to it, I tried not to think much about him at all.

*****

Louis Leopold Bianculli -- Luigi Leopoldo -- was born on the 17th of April, 1907, in the patch of lower Manhattan that then comprised Little Italy. After he died I ran across a crumbling birth certificate that identified his birthday as the 17th of May, but all of my life and most of his he celebrated it in April, so April it is. The document I found is possibly wrong. It's certainly, by this point, irrelevant.

He was born in a tenement at 5 Van Dam Street. Six or seven years later the family moved to King Street and there bounced around, building to building, floor to floor, until little Luigi's jobs started paying better and they were able to move uptown. His father, Carmine, was the son of a southern Italian couple that left for South America in the same late-19th-century wave of immigration that sent Europeans here. Carmine was born in Uruguay, then moved to New York City as a boy after his father -- my great-grandfather -- disappeared in South America, abandoning wife and kids. Maybe he was captured and killed by bandits; or maybe, as my father believed, he ran off to start another family. (At the height of his career Daddy received a letter from a South American woman named Bianculli who wanted to know whether he and she might possibly be related. He wrote back to say Sure, Yeah, We might be related -- my grandpa was a bigamist! To which she never responded. For which he was somewhat hurt. After which my mother pointed out that he had just called the woman a bastard.) Around 1900 or so Carmine married Achille Montesano, a delicately beautiful peasants' daughter who had fled a village near Naples, in sympathy and support of her illegitimately pregnant sister. She had such a beautiful voice that folks from around the neighborhood would visit to hear her sing.

I never met my father's parents but always imagined them sharing a deep and durable love -- "Achille, I am going, I am going," Carmine whispered from his deathbed late one night, and off he went. A copy of their wedding photo hangs above my staircase, and I regard it daily: he sitting, his swell of a mustache covering his cheeks; she standing, her right hand on his shoulder, her thin-boned figure an iron rod of determination. In her tiny, pointed features reside an expression of such ferocious Old World self-possession that I flinch when I look at her; I wonder what arguments she might have had with her scruffy American granddaughter. Maybe none. I don't speak Neapolitan, other than a couple of garbled folk songs, a handful of blasphemous curses invoking the Holy Family and one vulgar insult that identifies the recipient as a hard, dry nugget someone had a tough time voiding (STROOOONZZZ-a-CACAHHH-da-FOOOORRRRTS).

My father spoke Neapolitan exclusively until age five, after which he entered public school and his teachers told him to abandon his first language altogether. They actually told him to speak English at home, with his family, all the time, a doomed directive if there ever was one. Of course he ignored it, as most of his relatives neither spoke nor understood anything but a mellifluous southern dialect of Italian, and those who did speak English managed a bastardized version that involved the transmutation and elimination of entire syllables. Jer'city was his mother's word for Jersey City and other locales outside Manhattan. Californ' was her word for everywhere else. Vi'trol' was her word for Daddy, who distinguished himself early on as a prodigious blabber (Victrola). He came out talking and never stopped. The words gathered momentum as he rolled through life.

He was a good boy. I know this to be true because he told me he was a good boy, because Mama (who seemed to always have known him, even in childhood, even before she was born) told me he was a good boy, because I knew he could never have been anything but. He was studious and sad. A portrait from his childhood (was he six? seven?) shows an earnest boy with stiff posture and beautiful, wise dark eyes: comprehending and vigilant. During World War I he and his friends climbed the rooftops to look for invading Germans. He was poor, but everyone in Little Italy was poor. Most Christmases passed without a toy; one year a tenement neighbor gave him a tin bugle off a tree. Lou and his younger brother, Freddie, helped out where they could, taking odd jobs – for a wholesale druggist, for a women's corset company, for his Uncle Tony the suitmaker and Uncle Jimmy the safecracker -- to supplement the family income. Carmine worked in a candy factory and later on as an usher at Lewisohn Stadium. Years before she met Daddy, Mama knew his father as the small, stout man with the kind face and thick mustache who corralled people into seats before concerts.

Growing up, Louis swallowed books whole. He brought stacks of them home from the library. When he was a little bit older, and had a little bit of money, he brought stacks of them home from bookstores. He fell in love with Conrad, the ancient Greeks, Dante. He read and listened to 78s and listened to 78s and read and read some more and listened to more 78s. Books were a god; music was a god; as a child, at least, even God was a god. For a few years he planned on being a priest. Then an accountant. At night school he mastered shorthand, the ancient history of which became a lifelong fascination, and went to work for a subway expansion project that involved dynamiting a tunnel beneath Eighth Avenue. The city wanted to document the condition of all residences along the avenue in case some property owner thought to sue later on; the idea was to gather notes, in shorthand, on all buildings that were already partly demolished before the street went boom. For this my father was paid 30 or 40 bucks a week -- quite a salary in those days.

He made a good life for himself. He stayed out of trouble. He played handball. He boxed. He spent hours in the gym, sparred with friends and became a strapping young man with heavy shoulders and biceps he could bounce to the rhythm of a Tin Pan Alley song. He and his pals -- Dopey Dante, Alec, Big Lou Barba, who boxed professionally -- called themselves the Goof Club and vowed not to sleep around before marriage, hoping to avoid the clap. They were all good boys. Too bad Big Lou Barba went punch drunk, Daddy used to say, when he was long past remembering anything else. Too bad he had a glass jaw and took too many blows and lost his wits. Too bad.

By the time I knew him, Daddy couldn't watch a prize fight on television. All the Muhammad Ali fights I saw with Mama, who liked to watch him dance around the ring and make up sassy rhymes for the camera. Daddy wouldn't watch "Rocky" with us, and he wouldn't stand for anything in any movie or TV show that involved anyone throwing a punch to the head. Big Lou Barba went punch drunk, he'd say quietly, getting up to leave. I saw Big Lou Barba go punch drunk.

Alec was the one who shot himself. I never knew why – I never heard that story – but I understood that Daddy loved him deeply and saw in him something pure and real and maybe divine. After Alec killed himself Daddy went to a priest and asked him why. It's a lousy question to ask, but everyone asks it after a suicide, mainly because it's a good way to blow air around a room. Why. The priest should have said, "Who knows?" Or he should have said, "Sweet Jesus, it makes no sense to me." Or he should have said, "Stop asking questions, Louis, just go on home and get some sleep." But he didn't. He said, "Because it's God's will," and Daddy said, "Then I want nothing to do with God," and he had nothing to do with God for the next sixty-six years.

Or so he thought. Daddy would have howled if I'd said this to his face, but my darling apostate of a father sought and found and served the Almighty in his own way and time, though his way was crooked and his time was altogether dawdly. He was probably the most honest person I've ever known, the most generous and easily the least judgmental – as far as I could tell he never classed people, never judged them by their looks or education or station in life. Every stranger was a friend waiting to happen. He'd take aside a gas station attendant, ask his name, give him a snap derivation (first and last names), teach him a few phrases in his great-great-grandparents' native tongue and then force the guy to repeat what he'd learned two or three times until he got it right. "Say, you're a natural! I think you've got a gift for languages!" Daddy would say, even if the poor schmo had mangled it all. Then Daddy would squeeze his arm, wag a finger in his face and bless his new young friend in ancient Greek.

People loved him. He could wander into a drug store in a strange city, bring a pile of aspirin and cough drops and Fixident and whatnot up to the counter, banter delightedly with the lady at the register while the stuff was being rung up and then, digging absent-mindedly through his pockets, declare that he hadn't brought any money with him. See, his dear wife Jeanne was parked down the street and she had the cash, but he needed the aspirin right away because their daughter had a migraine, and he needed the cough drops right away because their other daughter had a terrible virus, and he needed the Fixident right away because his wife's dentures were banging around loose and making her gums bleed, and would the kind lady at the register mind if he just brought these things down to his family and got the money from his wife and then came back and paid? That would be all right? Yes? And what was the lady's name, or had she told him already? What's that? Say, that's Hungarian! What an unusual name! Do you speak any Hungarian? No? Can you say ASSZONY? Let me hear you say it, he'd say. Let me hear you say it -- ASSZONY, Hungarian for "woman"! Hey, that's good! Now, I leave you in peace – but not in pieces! – to bring these things to my wife and daughters, and I'll bring back that cash for you. All right? I'll just go right now. And before I leave, let me hear you say ISTENHOZZAD– that's Hungarian for "good-bye." ISTENHOZZAD!

He loved knowledge: Knowledge, for him, was the key to enlightenment, and he was evangelical in its cause. Robert C. Ruark, a colleague of his at the World-Telegram, once devoted an entire column to my father's intellectual and athletic pursuits, hypothesizing from the outset that "Maestro Louis Biancolli probably does not exist. He is a figment of my imagination, or else he has eight heads and is actually an incarnation of 'Information Please.' It should be impossible for anybody to be Louis Biancolli." He "rises early because there are so many words in the world and he cannot rest until he learns where they all came from." What's more, "He has attempted, in the past, to fill in the chinks in his day by teaching lessons in Spanish, Italian, French and Russian to his fellow staff-members on the paper, but most of us are so stupid thataway it is largely a waste of his time."

God bless my father, wherever he is. I imagine he's got a book cracked open somewhere – probably studying scripture, to which he never paid much attention in life (except as a language-learning tool), or maybe yakking it up with his brother Freddie. I know he's happy. After he died I had a contented dream in which I entered his hospital room to find him sitting bolt upright. As soon as I saw him he smiled and threw out his arms for a hug: "Aaaayyyymmmeeeeee, it's so good to see you!" He looked not as he did on his deathbed but about fifteen years younger, before his dementia had set in. "Daddy," I said, dumbfounded. "You're alive. But you were dead – I saw you. I touched you. You were dead." He smiled again, and even in my dream I felt I was close to tears. "Oh, I know," he said, hugging me once more. "But I'm fine now."

Another dream I had shortly before Christmas, seven or eight months after his death. In it I was walking through a busy holiday party in a darkened, festive, unfamiliar house. I entered a dimly lit hallway and caught sight of a peaceful old man, no one I recognized, standing quietly in the corner. In his arms he cradled a small baby. At first I paid no attention to the pair but then, drawn by his easy mien and his gentle manner with the baby, I approached. He looked up. I saw that it was Daddy. He held out the baby in his arms, smiled joyously and said, "This is the real miracle."

When I awoke I knew that the baby he held was Jesus. As many times as I've told the other dream to friends and family, I've held off telling this one – probably because of its overt religious content. I'm afraid of offending someone, or alienating someone, or giving someone the impression that I'm thumping Bibles with both fists and my forehead (and wasn't that a scene in "The Holy Grail"?). Or maybe I'm just afraid. At no other time have I ever dreamt of Jesus; I've never dreamt of God; as much as I admire mystics, I've never been one myself. The thought of encountering the Almighty in any form, dreamworld epiphany or otherwise, terrifies me. Yet the sight of my father with that blessed child was a vision almost mundane in its naturalness: Oh, yes. He's holding the baby Jesus. How sweet.

I took this to mean two things: That my father was okay, and that he had quite literally found peace with God after a lifetime of bitter and embattled questioning. Wishful thinking, skeptics might say, and they might be right; I do wish for my father nothing less than eternal love and contentment. But the act of wishing doesn't negate the fact of God's presence -- just because I want there to be an afterlife doesn't mean there isn't one. It's like the old saying: Just because I'm paranoid doesn't mean I'm not being followed. Or, in this case, following.

*****

By almost any standards, my father had a spectacular career. He entered journalism by way of boxing: Pitts Sanborn, the World-Telegram's chief music critic in the 1920s, bumped into Daddy in the gym. When he learned the young man knew shorthand, he offered him a job as his assistant. So Daddy took dictation for Sanborn's reviews, and eventually started writing them himself. By 1940 Sanborn had died and my father assumed the job of head critic. In that position he interviewed all the musical greats of the era; he hobnobbed with Leopold Stokowski and Eugene Ormandy; he welcomed Dmitri Shostakovich in Russian upon his arrival in the States (or, as Ruark put it, he "stalked up and hit him over the head in his own, difficult language"). There's no denying that Daddy enjoyed a significant four-decade career as one of the country's preeminent music critics -- there's no denying that he wrote and edited and co-wrote and co-edited books on opera and orchestral works, on Beethoven and Mozart, on Mary Garden, Kirsten Flagstad and Ruth Slenczynska -- there's no denying that he translated "The Divine Comedy" into luminescent blank verse (while he rode the subways!), that he nosed through libraries for years to come up with "Great Conversations," a thick compilation of dialogues between weighty historical figures, and that he ran himself ragged by covering bits and pieces of two, three, four concerts a night.

For 38 years, from 1928 to 1966, he wrote for the World-Telegram. He was regarded by performers and colleagues alike as a prince among critics -- a decent, gifted man who didn't forget there were human beings behind the music. He never wanted to ruin someone's career. He never assumed he had the power. If a concert or individual work was flawed, he said so, sometimes with trenchant humor, but if it was catastrophically awful he declined to review it at all. When you attend two or three performances a day you can afford to ignore a bomb.

In the 40s he served as annotator for the New York Philharmonic. In the 50s he interviewed Casals, wrote record-jacket copy, appeared on "Opera Quiz" in his light-toned, chatty tenor (I have a tape). In the 60s he reviewed the Beatles in Carnegie Hall; he called them "four characters in search of a barber" and compared the squalling girls in attendance to bacchantes and Corybantes "in wild Greek rites." As ever he wrote with breezy learnedness, mixing a lively conversational style with daunting scholarship and gem-like poetic turns. His writing was above all emotional, inclined to hyperbole and fearless in its defense of beauty. Consider one of my father's last articles for the World-Telegram -- an April 14, 1966 review of the Boston Symphony Orchestra, conducted by Erich Leinsdorf.

The BSO performed two symphonies that night: Mozart's A Major, No. 29, and Brahms' Second. Regarding the Mozart, he wrote:

> One seemed face to face with the 18-year-old genius who in a moment of illumination in 1774 fashioned a masterpiece that is as close to

perfection as anything can be.   Leinsdorf
recaptured the moment.
If there is music more exquisite and dreamlike than
the Andante I somehow missed it this season. It
moves on tiptoed thoughts. . . .

Of the two (symphonies), Brahms' is perhaps the
greater music, and Mozart's the greater miracle.
The kinship, other than the lyric rapture at the heart
of both, was the utmost refinement and feeling of
last night's playing.

When I read a passage like this I feel awed and
proud -- and envious. He did this on *deadline*? Why can't *I*
write this way on deadline? ("It moves on tiptoed
thoughts" -- where'd that line come from? Can I have it?) I
have so few memories of him at his typewriter, pounding
away, that I take special delight in his writing -- it's a
delight that combines the familiar with the undiscovered,
like running across a long-unopened letter from an old
friend. Louis Biancolli was an accomplished critic, but I
didn't know him at the height of his career. That father, the
other father, the father who wasn't forgetful and old and
nutty, seemed always so far away.

His career didn't matter to me. Or it mattered, but
not in the way his smile mattered, or the delight in his eyes
when he recognized a loved one, or the lilting cadence to
his greetings. Some say senility kills a man before his
death, but I disagree: I believe it distills him to his most
essential self. Illness and aging burn off all that's
irrelevant, leaving behind only what isn't. In my father's
case, his generosity never left him. His ebullience never
left him. Neither did his need to comprehend.

When I think of my father's death, I think of the
weeks preceding it as a crash lesson in spirituality, like a
quickie prep course for the SATs. Even in his final years,
he didn't lose his desire to learn and felt compelled to ask
question after blurry question -- often on trivialities,

sometimes to the irritation of friends and family -- in his will to understand. His age, condition and apartness from the world meant he understood little. But he wanted to; it was his nature; he felt somehow derelict when his once-powerful intellect began to fail him. Of all the indignities of aging, this one, I think, was the hardest. He knew enough to know what he had lost. This is not to say he lost himself -- despite our cultural temptation to dismiss Alzheimer's patients (and other mentally or intellectually compromised people) as somehow less than fully human, he was as much Louis at the end of his life as he was in the robust middle of it. More so: The grand loop had brought him back to the beginning, the point from which all of us arrive and depart. He came from God and would go to God. It was the nearness that made him whole.

*****

And now, a word about that suicide thing. (Or is it a suicide *thang*? Can suicide be a *thang*?)

There are dozens, no, hundreds, no, thousands of books out there on successful parenting, tracts on discipline and self-esteem and health and sleep-pattern-development (verb: to FERBER) and Attachment Parenting and Hyper Parenting and poop. Lots of books on poop. But what none of them properly addresses is the one hard and fast rule to which anybody having a child absolutely must adhere. Namely: Don't try to kill yourself. If you can manage to get through a kid's formative years without taking a near-lethal dose of sleeping pills, well, then -- Huzzah! Job well done! Lean forward, and I'll pin a medal around your well-deserving, remarkably preserved chest. You've passed the only test that's required of you -- the only test that my father, despite all the love and good intentions in the world, totally flunked.

I was eleven when it happened. When he did it. When he woke from a nap, entered a psychotic fugue state, believed my mother had left him for another man, and tried to kill himself. He swallowed Seconal, about fifty of them, enough to kill a horse. More than enough to kill a Daddy. But it didn't. For some sneaky incomprehensible Godly reason he snapped-to after downing the pills, perceived the horror of what he'd done and stumbled downstairs to find Mama. She, realizing that she could not carry a 180-pound man into a car, told her husband to get outside and climb into the Corolla while he was still conscious. By the time she joined him he was comatose.

And so he remained, for nine days. And so began the single most significant trauma of his life and, for seventeen years, mine.

I saw him there, plugged into rubber tubes, puffed and shiny like a paraffin doll. Attached to a respirator, he breathed In. Out. In. Out. Lucy and I walked in and saw him and stood there and stood there and stood there and said nothing and then, when Mama beckoned, walked out. All the while his plastic breathing. Out. In. Out. In. Mama said she wanted us to see him and know he was comatose and know he might die and know he hadn't just disappeared, boom, poof, in a cotton-white cloud of smoke. So we saw him; we knew; we couldn't escape knowing, wouldn't escape knowing, for the rest of our living days. My bouncy puffy papa is fixed in my mind's restless eye; I've written many poems about it, most of them bad. In one I imagine him as a balloon. I stick a pin in him and he pops, flap-flap-flapping around the room. Bounce a papa stick a papa watch a papa pop. Pop pop pop. Watch a papa pop.

I don't remember much of what I felt, at that time, about my father. I'm sure I felt anger or hatred or betrayal, possibly all three. But I don't remember. One thing I do remember is sitting in the back seat of a black Lincoln Continental driven by my best friend's mom. A month earlier Tonya's dad had been killed in a construction accident. I sat in the left rear seat behind her mother, who minutes before had told me that Daddy had "swallowed too much medicine," that Mama was with him at the hospital, that Lucy had gone home with her best friend, Dolly, and that I was going to spend the night and maybe the next couple of days at Tonya's. Tonya sat to the right of me. It was nighttime, and it was raining, and as I stared into the cold wet blackness I felt my will to object – to Daddy's hospitalization, to my not having pajamas or a toothbrush or my security blanket, to the obscene injustice of the thing – drain away. The events of the world fell around me like a soft rain. "Are you scared?" Tonya asked, and I shook my head no. "I would be," she said – speaking three of the kindest words anyone has ever said to me, before or since. I said nothing in reply, but felt relieved: I was allowed to be scared. Only then did it occur to me that Daddy might die.

*****

At first I didn't realize that he'd tried to kill himself. Lucy knew. I'm sure I knew, too, on some level – Mama had certainly given me all the pertinent details. She told me he had taken an overdose of medicine. She told me he had taken a HUGE overdose of medicine. She told me that if he hadn't come to his senses, if he hadn't recognized what he'd done and gone to Mama in terror and crawled into the Corolla by himself, he would have died. I knew this, see. I knew this, and yet Mama had never used the phrase "suicide attempt," and I certainly never thought of it myself. I understand the omission: Mama's philosophy in all manners of life and teaching was to bombard us with facts, then sit back and watch the effect. If we were ready to understand something, we would understand it. If we weren't, we wouldn't. Simple. She took this approach with sex education (we received exhaustive instruction from age two onward; think diagrams), with cooking, with time management, with our general deportment -- everything. So it certainly follows that when it came to Daddy's suicide attempt, she would give us the blow-by-blow info and wait and see if we got it. Lucy got it. I didn't.

I don't remember when I made sense of Mama's facts. I suppose it was a matter of finding the words and then being able to say them. Once Daddy had pulled out of his coma (Nine days, was that it, Jeannie? A nine-day coma?) he was more or less forced to enter a psychiatric hospital, and I was more or less forced to admit that he was there because he wasn't quite right in the head. "Her father's in a MENTAL INSTITUTION," a classmate announced, in my presence and in the presence of an embarrassed and sympathetic teacher. I felt no ill will toward the kid; he was right. Daddy was then in the middle of a six-month stay at a private psych program, and although he seemed normal during our weekend visits with him – although the hospital looked more like a college campus than a cobwebby-gothic insane asylum – I was alarmed by its prohibition of knives and razors. Nothing freaked me out more than the fact that Mama had to buy Daddy an electric shaver. Still, he seemed happy there. He responded to therapy. He had breakthroughs with his shrink. We met with the man during a family counseling session, during which I told both Daddy and his doctor that I wanted to be allowed to ride my bicycle on the road around Lake Waramaug; to my amazement, he agreed, for once regarding his own over-protectiveness as somehow pathological. Daddy vowed never to take sleeping pills again (he didn't). He vowed to learn to drive (he tried; after twice almost-crashing the car and once blowing a gasket, he gave up). While in the hospital he watched films ("The Wizard of Oz"! What a marvelous movie!), made art (including a cheeky little rabbit sculpture), bought piles of gifts for his "dames" (notepads and organizers with pin-thin two-inch pencils were a favorite) and stuffed hard candy into his pockets for distribution on daily strolls. The other patients liked him – they called him "candy man" and found in his off-kilter cheer some cause for joy in darkness. One young man there truly loved him, lit up like a bulb when he saw him and bought him a present – an Elton John LP, the one with "Your Song" – when he left. I don't remember his name. But I remember the smile that cracked his long, weary face as Daddy plumbed his trousers for a mint.

My father, for his part, was oblivious; he didn't notice when people loved him. So we had to say it a lot: Daddy I love you, Daddy I love you, Daddy I love you. Often he fished for reassurance (How I love you, girls! I love you! Did I hear – did I hear a reply? Did I hear it? Say it: I. Love. You. Dad-dy!), and he almost always got it. He needed to have it spelled out for him. Otherwise he would never have noticed, just as he never noticed nine-tenths of what happened to him. One summer morning he stuck his hand into a whirring lawnmower, almost severing his thumb at the knuckle. But he thought nothing of it – that little thing? Naaaaaah, I don't need a doctor. Getting him to the emergency room proved difficult, requiring much loud persuasion on Mama's part (LOUIS LOUIS LOUIS DO YOU WANT TO LOSE YOUR THUMB); getting him to postpone a speaking engagement later that evening proved impossible. So he went, his half-severed finger bundled in gauze, and about mid-way through the speech he flung his hand onto the table in a moment of emphatic Southern Italian arm-wagging, opening the wound and punctuating the speech with blood. He didn't notice; his horrified audience had to tell him. He was heedless of himself.

*****

> Come to me my melancholy baby,
> Cuddle up and don't be blue.
> All your fears are foolish fancies may be,
> You know, dear, that I'm in love with you.
> Ev'ry cloud must have a silver lining,
> Wait until the sun shines through.
> Smile my honey dear,
> While I kiss away each tear,
> Or else I shall be melancholy too.

*****

Daddy always knew when somebody else had died. He knew when his best friend Ted had died. He knew when Freddie had died. Both times he snatched the words from my mouth before I had a chance to say them; with his brother, he knew from the second the phone rang. "Freddie's dead," he said, his shoulders slumping at the kitchen table. When Lucy died, Daddy was living in a nursing home at the time -- he'd been there since Mama's catastrophic near-death (she was always having catastrophic near-deaths) a year earlier -- and although we visited him after the suicide, we were resolute in not telling him about it. We certainly didn't drag him to the burial. But at the very moment Lucy's ashes were being interred under a tree twelve miles away, Daddy scuffed up to a nurse's station near his room, agitated out of his wits. "I sense that someone has died," he said. "Has someone died?" No, they lied. And then he scuffed away.

He was psychic, in some ways. At carnivals we steered him over to the pick-a-number booths, where he invariably picked the right one: I still have the oversized patchwork velveteen turtle (purple-N-orange-N-pink) that he won for Lucy at the Bridgewater Fair. As a young man he was always saving people – from a burning house, from a flood – usually because he happened to poke his nose around a corner or out the window or around the bend at just the right moment. And he recognized, without fail, the moments when I was suffering from some silent anguish (boys; my period; my body; boys), approaching me at just the right moment with a kind word or a piece of candy. He just knew: It was intuition, or the urge to connect, or love. Daddy understood people even when he'd lost his memory of who they were. During the last year of his life he made daily rounds through the nursing home, asking everyone's name (he always forgot), cheering everyone up. He immediately sensed which among his fellow residents needed the biggest dose of Louis, and he provided it in spades. "And what's your name again?" he'd ask. "Did you know that means 'God is great'?"

Every day of my childhood Daddy would head out
the door for long walks down the lake road and into town,
his arms going swirl-pump-swing-swirl-pump-swing to the
waltz of Swedish calisthenics, his open, dark-eyed face
exploding in smiles for every retiree and jogger and
vacationer and gardening lady and kid on a bike that he
met along the way. "Hello! Beautiful day! Hello! Hello!,"
he'd yell, and sometimes he'd treat them to his rendition of
"Melancholy Baby" in Neapolitan. They all loved him, and
why not? Everyone loved him: Not once in my life have I
bumped into a friend or former acquaintance of old Lou
who didn't canonize him as the world's most unpretentious
and giving man. As a critic he gave concert tickets to
impoverished music lovers. As an old ex-boxer he offered
bag-punching lessons to every child in the neighborhood,
and swore up and down that "girls are the best" at catching
the rhythm (THUMP-a-da THUMP-a-da THUMP-a-da
went the bag, and the porch, and the house). And he could
not pass a piece of litter without stooping to pick it up – he
was always worried that a barefoot child would cut her
foot on a broken bottle, or that the ice cream wrappers
crumpled on the road's sandy shoulder would mar
someone's view of the lake. By the time he returned home
from his walks his hands were filled with trash.

At breakfast he piled dried fruit and yogurt into his
All-Bran, called it "Daddy's Combo Cereal" and tried to
get everyone else to eat it, as though his children wouldn't
be caught dead within thirty-five yards of a prune. "Try it!
It's delicious!" he implored, proffering tablespoons of dark
fibrous material swimming in yogurt. "No, Daddy, No!"
we yelled, recoiling from the offensive flatware. "BUT
IT'S DELICIOUS!" he said. "BUT WE BELIEVE YOU!"
we told him. "AND IT'S SO GOOD FOR YOU!" he said.
"AND WE KNOW!" we affirmed. And so on and so forth,
ad infinitum, ad nauseum, ad Louis.

He was a magic man, with a magic touch: Even his
pockets were magic, filled with rubber bands and safety

pins and stamps and money and pens and pencils and paper clips and tiny notepads for jotting down random thoughts on word origins. "Daddy, can I have a rubber band?" I'd ask him, breathless from some childish errand. "Let's just check my magic pocket," he'd reply, reaching in and pulling out a cupped hand piled with smallish knick-knacks. There, at the top, would be the needed item – along with a butterscotch candy that Daddy would offer, and I would take, marveling at his endless supplies.

He was not a traditional father. He was old; he was odd; he was idle; he had a temper. When I was two he kicked a hole in the wall of our Queens flat after Lucy and I spilled our chocolate milk (Bosco, the NesQuick of yesteryear) simultaneously and just as simultaneously bonked our heads under the kitchen table trying to clean it up. In his strangest moments he faked heart attacks or said we were trying to kill him or threatened (what else) to kill himself. Probably he was manic; certainly he was depressed. All the same he never struck us, never swore at us, never slapped or threatened or shamed us, never did anything other than love us in his own, unorthodox way. Mama and Daddy vowed early on never to hit us, and they didn't; we weren't even spanked. The pacifist-reformed-pugilist-gun-control-advocate wanted nothing of violence. He wanted nothing of hatred, or pain, or illness. That he inflicted all three on himself (and, indirectly, on us) was an ironic blow from which he never fully recovered.

When I was young he slept a lot. I accepted this as a fact of life, as all children accept their parents' oddities – why he slept a lot I didn't question. I was more or less accustomed to the sight of him lying in bed face down, bombed on sleeping pills, a pile of Indo-European etymological books on the nightstand beside him. He had retired young, when he was 59 and I was two and a half: He simply never returned at the end of the 1966 New York City newspaper strike. If he had returned to work for just one month he would have earned a pension, but he refused, one of those random inexplicable facts that dot his life and

mine. The Daily News even offered to hire him for four or
five weeks, just so he'd qualify for a Guild pension, but he
wouldn't do it. I don't know why he wouldn't do it. Mama
didn't know why he wouldn't do it. Maybe he didn't know
why he wouldn't do it. He had some reason. Or maybe no
reason at all.

Unlike Lucy, who tagged along once or twice on
his beat, I had no memory of him as a working stiff. To me
he was just Daddy, the guy in bed, the guy with the elegant
muscular hands and permanent beret. (A black one, a gift
from my mother, who for years afterward wished she'd
never bought it. He put it on his head in the late 1960s and
didn't take it off for fifteen years. Perchance I hyperbolize.
He may well have removed the thing, to sleep or scratch or
bathe or comb, but if so, I never witnessed it. As far as I
knew he kept it on his head without break until well into
the Reagan administration. I'm not sure how or why he
finally got rid of it; probably Mama swiped it off his head
when he wasn't looking, threw it on the floor, stomped on
it, autoclaved it, stuck it with pins, mashed it with a ball-
peen hammer and burned the remains in a bonfire.) As a
child I was aware of his career only as a collection of feats
-- as a neat but static line-up of leather-bound books in the
living-room secretary. He wrote some stuff, he knew some
people, he told some stories about Kirsten Flagstad and
Mary Pickford (he ghosted her memoir) and the time he
visited the set of "Rear Window" (What -- no clothes lines,
boys? A New York City tenement ought to have clothes
lines!), but so what? It was his stash of chocolate I cared
about. Daddy, can I have some? Suuuuure, suuuuure,
Amigita, suuuuure. But don't tell Mommy! It's almost
supper time! I hear his voice so clearly, this Daddy of
mine; I can't always recall Lucy's or Mama's, but Daddy's
is always with me, silken and sing-song and filled with
questioning pain.

*****

At the end of the day, behind closed doors, he and Mama yelled. About what I never knew. In the last decade or so the fighting waned to nil, no doubt because of Daddy's dementia -- a blessing of sorts -- and a gradually acquired habit of sleeping from 7 p.m. to 3 a.m. He just wasn't awake long enough to get into scraps with his wife. But during my childhood my parents argued often and loudly, usually at night. Sometimes Lucy would pad into my room and we would sit awake, staring at the crack of light under Daddy's door, waiting for them to stop. They always did. And when they did, Mama came into my room and hugged us and kissed us and said We're Done Fighting Now Girls and Daddy and I Love You and Daddy and I Love Each Other Too and Don't Worry Don't Worry Everything's Fine. I believed her when she said Everything's Fine; Lucy didn't. I never doubted that my parents loved each other – I never doubted that they'd always be together. Incredible as it sounds (and the older I get, the less credible it seems), the possibility of divorce never crossed my mind, not even once. The knot that bound my parents just looked too tangled to break: It was convoluted to the point of inviolacy. There was an illogic to it, a sense of people behaving irrationally. Against all reason they believed in their marriage; they believed in their wedding vows, long after the Groom had tanked himself on Seconal. In sickness and in health. In music and in discord. In madness and in sense. Amen.

*****

In all the time I've been working on this book, I've tried to find just the right word for "crazy." There are plenty of synonyms: cracked, harebrained, deranged, barmy, marbles, bananas (ooooh: shades of Lucy in the kitchen), schizoid, loony-tunes, maniacal, nuts, bats, bonkers, screwy, daft, demented, weird, cockeyed, addlebrained, crackers, flaky, wacko, and Not Of This Earth. At different times different members of my family qualified as one or all of the above. But the problem, in finding the right word for my father, is that his mental instability -- his disconnectedness from the outside world -- was so unimportant to everyone who loved him. Yes, he was a nut, but the word "nut" doesn't convey the genius and charity and gentle-giant goodness of the man. He had a jumbo heart. "Your father is a kind man -- always remember that," Mama said more than once, most often when I was grousing about his infirmity or strangeness. Even when he was acting crazy, he was a loving man acting crazy, and that's tacitly different from a hate-filled man acting the same way.

I don't believe he ever knew what a good man he was. He never knew what he had accomplished with his books, his abundant love, his trilling joy in meeting people. I doubt he ever saw the light he cast around him. Had he, he wouldn't have tried to kill himself. (Maybe.) The biggest mystery of my childhood was the depth of his self-loathing and his tendency to celebrate everyone's accomplishments but his own. For that reason I never hated him. Or if I did, I got it out of my system early on, deciding, at some point, that he was a decent man and all in all an extraordinary father. Besides, he hated himself: He never forgave himself for attempting suicide, so it seemed redundant for me to hate him, too. One person's unrelenting odium was enough. In my mid-20s, while some of my peers were busy being self-righteously furious at their parents (Mother Denied Me The: Breast/Car Keys/Hostess Cupcakes/Freedom to Be Myself), one of them would periodically wonder why I wasn't at mine. I told them I'd done that already – I didn't have the energy for it any longer. After a while it becomes easier simply to love. ("My yoke is easy, and my burden light,'' said Jesus, and once I realized he was talking about love – once I realized that's all he was ever talking about, love – I began to listen.)

Love was the only gospel that my heathen-atheistic-perma-bereted-prune-eating father could bring himself to teach. It was his god – his God, though he took a long time seeing It – and on that subject he evangelized, with eloquence and zeal. He loved largely. He loved indiscriminately and foolishly, seeing only good in people or, if he saw bad, not responding to it. Had he believed his love had come from God he would have loved God, too. 'Yet long after I and Mama and Lucy began to believe, we recognized Daddy's huge compassion as an expression of faith beyond the frustrated utopian urges of a lapsed radical. It came from the same well as God's – and in its own way, his love, all "secular" love, was drawn from the same divine source. He loved God and didn't know it, or didn't want to. To love is to connect ourselves with the Almighty, just as swimming on a beach in Maine (if you can stand the cold) connects us to the coast of Ireland. Thus I was reared in a family that worshiped God in action and substance but not in semantics, not in pronouns, not in name. There were no Yous or Hims or Hes or Thous, no crosses in the house, no grace before meals, no talk of Jesus except as a good man that some people (Other People) believe was divine (But We Don't), no jaunts to church except for weddings or funerals or those awkward unforeseen occasions when a friend or relative schlepped us along. None of that. But my parents gave us love; and by giving us love, they sent us, unwittingly, to the fountainhead.

*****

The atheist and the agnostic were devout believers in the power of compassion. They were devout believers in pluralism. They were devout believers in music, literature, voting, Scrabble, Hubert Humphrey and dessert. They told us not to judge by skin color, not to value money above all, not to condemn the Russians for being communists, not to condemn the poor for being poor, not to hit, not to hunt (every fish I ever caught I tossed back to be re-caught another day, until some had gaping holes in their mouths),

not to stand mute before sexist taunts, not to tell ethnic
jokes, not to have sex before marriage, not to drink, not to
do drugs, not to glorify the second amendment, not to
glorify the death penalty, not to glorify war, not to fret too
much over broken or lost things ("they're not alive!"), not
to drive large clunky automatic cars (I do anyway; sorry,
Ma), not to fear the city, not to go bra-less, not to be rude,
and not to let the hosts wash the dishes after you've eaten
supper at someone's house. They were moral conservatives
and social liberals, an unusual combination in any era;
there was something Dorothy Day-ish about them, minus
the Catholicism. Daddy in particular would have made a
fine Catholic Worker, what with his socialist background
and abhorrence of material froufrou. Had he lived another
life, he might have been one.

They never told us not to believe in God. They just
said, We Don't. They said, You Decide For Yourselves,
Girls, not realizing we would and they would, too, and
damned if we didn't all eventually agree. Did I say
damned? Damned and blessed, cursed and chosen. When I
hear someone bemoaning the plight of the un-Godly, the
un-churched, the irreligious, the lapsed souls, the
misguided, the pagan masses or the secular humanists –
when I hear someone say They're Wrong, or They're Lost,
or They Need God, or They Must Be Saved – when I hear
that, I have three immediate and concurrent thoughts. One
is, Well, of course they're lost. Aren't we all lost? Don't
we all need God? The second is, Give them time; God
knows what path they're treading better than you do. And
the third is, Why do all televangelists have bad hair?

Grace is a curious gift. It is at once transparent and
mysterious, like a prism: I'm awestruck at its beauty, but
I'm not sure how it works. Why was I given the grace to
know God, and others weren't? Surely I didn't ask for it.
After Tonya's father died I sometimes went to Mass with
her family, and I never felt anything but bored. In an art
class I made a grim purple-and-black "recruitment poster"
mocking nuns ("Tired of loud colors? . . . Get cramps

trying to smile?''). After Lucy converted I was perplexed by her unrelenting goodness; she winced, once, when I used the word "suck," and I wound up yelling at her for being such a vexatious goody-goody (Jesus CHRIST Lucy you don't even SWEAR). I never wanted to be that holy. Yet God led me to believe. God led me to believe, and not another. I don't know why, just as I don't know why I can bend my thumbs behind my knuckles. Why I was born with brown eyes while Lucy was born with blue. Why.

When I was ten years old, Daddy mowed straight into a yellow jackets' nest hidden in the brush under a birch tree. The roused yellow jackets stung him around forty times, an assault I recall for its vehemence, for the fact that my father didn't swell up like a dirigible, and for the baking-soda plasters my mother applied laboriously to each angry welt. He was covered in pasty white polka dots -- his legs, his arms, his face, his back, his neck. I knew as I watched Mama apply her doubtful medicine, just as I knew when I saw him nesting in tubes in the I.C.U., that he had been spared. I knew that he might have died. I knew that God might have taken him though I didn't know I believed in God. I knew grace when I saw it; or maybe I called it luck. But I sensed, with the unerring, inarticulate sensitivity of a child, the caprice in his recovery and the wordless question that begged to be asked. I sensed the Why.

*****

There are many things I never knew about my father. I never knew when, why or how he became a socialist. I never knew when he stopped being one, though I always suspected he was done in by Stalin. I never knew when the United States Government started opening his mail, though I saw it myself and recall being told never, ever, to discuss Daddy's political history with anyone at any time. I never knew when or why he changed the family

name from "Biaculli" to "Biancolli," though he liked to
say he did it to avoid seeing it misspelled as "Bianculi"
(minus an "L"), an alteration that changes the meaning
from "white hills" (bianco / culli) to, how shall I put this,
"white butts" (bianco / culi). I never knew his favorite
symphony, or his favorite opera, or his favorite conductor.
I never knew what drove him to write so many books, or
review so many concerts. I never knew when or why he
became a lifelong teetotaler. I never knew when he stopped
eating bread and pasta, though he must have consumed
them in his youth and certainly bumped into said items
while writing restaurant reviews under the byline Barclay
Hudson (after the World-Telegram's street address; he
sacrificed his gallbladder to some marathon eating duel
with a rival critic). I never knew when or why he stopped
traveling, or why he refused to accept a year-long
fellowship in London. I never knew why he didn't attend
my high school (or college, or grad school) graduation. I
never knew how he chipped his tooth.

On the other hand, I do know that:

1) He loved a good, mushy love song;

2) This included "Feelings";

3) He loved coffee;

4) He once tried to make cappuccino by shaking a
thermos until it exploded upward, leaving coffee stains on
the kitchen ceiling that were *never, ever* cleaned (please
note italics);

5) He taught me how to play five-card stud but had
no poker face whatsoever;

6) During World War II he volunteered to
parachute into Italy as a spy (see: ". . . no poker face
whatsoever," above) but was rejected because of an old leg
injury;

7) He came close to getting his socialist neck slit
open during a shave by an Italian-American barber with
fascist sympathies;

8) He had a crush on Mary Pickford;

9) Every year he got Christmas cards from: Mary

Pickford and her husband, Buddy Rogers; and Leonard Bernstein;

10) He once used "f----in' " on the phone with an editor, prompting Lucy to say "Please pass the f----in' milk" for a month;

11) He ate so much chocolate while writing books that he owned two sets of clothes, one pre-book, one post-;

12) He had a crush on Mary Tyler Moore;

13) He "loved the ladies";

14) Before walking down the hill to pick up the post, he announced without fail that he was "going to get the mail -- but not the female";

15) Before leaving a room occupied by one or more persons, he announced without fail that he would "leave you in peace -- but not in pieces";

16) He never cheated on my mother;

17) He never hit me or Lucy;

18) He never got sick (except for, you know, being clinically depressed and trying to kill himself -- oops); and finally,

19) He never lied.

*****

My father, a fighter to the last, Big Lou Barba's sparring partner and a man of mulish stick-to-it-ive-ness, had a hard time facing his own timely demise. "A hundred or bust!" he'd say, determined to live a century. Clearly, he didn't want to die (though action and word said otherwise), but he just as clearly didn't want to give up control over the whens and hows. He hated the idea that his body and mind might (did) break down without his say-so. And he was downright panicky about us: If he'd had his way, he would have kept the three of us in vacuum-sealed mason jars on the kitchen table, right alongside the marmalade and multivitamins. "Your father's a worry wart," Mama would say, but he was more than that; he was a free-floating-angst-in-search-of-a-target wart. He lived in fear that one of us might spontaneously ignite (or get hit by a car, or get abducted by Sasquatch, or get tangled in seaweed and drown) on an afternoon walk to the mailbox. He lived in fear that *he* might spontaneously ignite on an afternoon walk to the mailbox. My guess is he felt relief every time he didn't.

Failed radical that he was, Daddy wanted to believe in the solid world around him: In his health, in his family, in the liberal causes that kept him engaged in politics even when he'd lost all faith in politicians. When you don't believe in another world this one takes on a terrible primacy. He used to say he worshiped music and those who make it, and I think he did; his adulation of Beethoven was a kind of religion, a bit like the Elvis cult without all the Day-Glo folk art. He worshiped Nature, too; he worshiped the Lake and the hills that hugged it, declaring it once and again the most beautiful spot on Earth. And he worshiped us -- Mama in particular. She was his reluctant savior.

Conversion, so often characterized as a change in heart, was in my father's case a change in sight. He saw things differently: himself, his life, his loved ones, death. The "fantastic expansion" he spoke of was in fact a realization that every corner of his world was ignited and infused with love. The corners themselves had not changed; he only saw them as they'd been all along. He looked in one direction and saw a shaft of light. He looked in another and saw Lucy. He looked upward, finally upward, and saw the fulgent mysteries around him, mysteries that had lain in wait for decades and now rejoiced to be discovered.

*****

On a shelf in my living room sits a 3 x 5 photo, black and white, circa 1945, of a man in a snap-brim hat. He is smashingly handsome: vital, laughing, in his late 30s or early 40s, his curved Roman nose anchoring the heavy features of his face. His arms are crossed; his hat is tipped; his bow-tie is sassy, polka-dotted and crisp.

It is approaching ten years since my father died, and I am still transfixed by his photo. I am transfixed not because I see it some soft reminder of the man I knew, but because I see no reminder at all. He isn't there. I regard it as I might the candid shot of a golden-era movie star, some distant but intriguing personality whose charisma gripped the camera and commandeered passage to the present day. Who was this? I ask myself, studying his smile and seeing in it vague hints of my own. What was he doing? Was he at work? Out on the town? And why was he laughing? Whoever he was, whatever he meant to the people who knew him, the man in the photo had disappeared years before I learned he was ever there. Only now, in the long years since his death, have I started to get to know him.

My father was 56 when I was born. Two and a half years later, he retired, leaving behind almost four decades with the World-Telegram. He'd been highly regarded in music and newspaper circles, admired for his lively prose and his reluctance – even refusal – to write a vitriolic review. He was known for his scholarship, his athleticism, his fascination with linguistics, his generosity, his Italian roots, his love of opera, the baker's dozen of books he'd published, his amateur boxing and his manic, heavy-handed way with a typewriter. He had a reputation for busting manuals.

The man I knew was older, frailer, less sure of himself and the world. He was 85 when he died, and the last fifteen years had been difficult and slow. Alzheimer's or some other undiagnosed form of senile dementia (was it brain damage from his coma?) had nibbled away at his memory and made it first uncomfortable, then impossible for him to keep up with friends who knew him in his prime. He stopped writing. He stopped listening to music. After a while he even stopped reading, focusing all of his mental energy on crossword puzzles. When I went away to college I wrote him long and frequent letters, and he did his best to respond – always in huge, block-like handwriting, rarely more than a page. Some time later he ceased trying, just as he had ceased trying to keep up with the conversations that whirled around him like fallen leaves on a windy day. He forgot faces, names, ideas. He forgot the first half of a sentence by the time he'd heard the last.

My father never knew me as an adult. In his final years, while I was thrashing out a career in journalism, he was receding further and further behind the divider. I longed to tell him about my work, about the changes in the newspaper industry since he'd retired, about my breathless explorations into new writers and composers. I wanted to tell him about myself – who I was, what sort of woman I'd become, who my friends were and what my life was – but I couldn't. I was Amy, Amigita, his little friend from long ago. I was not the person who grew up and went to college and graduate school and got married and found her greatest professional joy doing almost exactly what her father had done for a living. I was the daughter who loved him – that was enough, and that was all. The rest he forgot. Even my husband, whom he greatly admired, was greeted always as a kind but nameless gentleman, that strong young man who appeared with his daughter and enveloped him in hugs. In my father's eyes, it was all a blur. And so was I.

I wasn't there when he died. For weeks after the fall that broke his hip I drove back and forth, Albany to Connecticut, Connecticut to Albany, fearing that every visit with him would be my last. We knew he was dying and said goodbye many times. Only half aware, his attention fixed firmly on the next world, he accepted our farewells in silence and awaited the end with sweet-natured distraction. When it came I was at a friend's housewarming party in Albany, chatting about music in the fresh heat of a June sun. My husband, who had gone home to do some work, returned earlier than expected and quietly pulled me aside. He said the words and I cried, then told my father that I loved him and thanked God for him and hoped he was all right. It felt odd to address him directly and know that everything I said would, at last, be understood. He wouldn't forget a word.

In the days that followed I spoke to him more and more. Late one night before the funeral I left my parents' house and sat on the damp, cool lawn, watching ripples of light skate across the lake below. I thought of my father, not of his last days, but of the man I'd glimpsed as a child before he retreated into the fog. I remembered that father. I remembered the fears I'd shared with him, the arguments we'd had, the interest he once took in my life and the pleasure that crossed his face when I snagged a baseball from the air and threw it swiftly back. ("One-hand bip!" he'd yell, using a name he had earned as a youngster. "Look at that! One-hand bip!")

That night I told him everything. I told him about my husband, our wedding, the rewards and challenges since then. I told him about my work as an arts writer; I told him how proud I was to be his daughter and how often people I interviewed asked me if I was related to "the New York critic. . . Louis Biancolli." I told him about my love of music, which had exploded since his Alzheimer's had taken hold, and I described the hard but happy task of learning the violin. I told him I played in an orchestra and taught writing part-time at a nearby college. I told him I liked to jog, and bike, and feel my own strength, as he did at my age. I told him about the novel I'd written, the new work I'd started, the movies I'd seen, the books I'd read and the eccentricities I'd developed. I told him I had a gray streak in my hair. I told him my friends seemed to value me and I liked to make them laugh. I told him I'd inherited his taste for chocolate. I liked to eat. I liked to dance. I tried to be a good Catholic. I loved my mother and husband. I missed my sister. I missed him.

Did he hear me? I believe so, yes. And he heard me on many occasions that followed, as I huddled over my reporter's notebook in one concert hall or another, trying to find just the right word to describe that pianist's phrasing.

Daddy, help me. " `Fluid,' Amigita. Write `fluid,' " he says, or I say to myself in the voice I'm always able to conjure. And as the months and years go by it's a younger voice, a stronger voice. I look at an empty seat two rows ahead and I imagine him sitting there -- alert, focused, his hair the salt and pepper of my childhood, not the thick white brush that I last saw. He is an old man no longer.

Bit by bit, I am forming a new relationship with my father. It hasn't been easy; for years I had treated him not as a fellow adult but as a child, as someone less capable than I, less aware, less equipped to cope with the world and its byzantine rules. And I hated it. I will never forget my father's second cataract operation, when he returned from the hospital bandaged and blind and warned, by his doctors, not to lean over under any circumstances. If he did, the tiny stitches holding in his eye's new lens would pop, rendering him permanently sightless. I had taken off the week to help my mother, and between the two of us we held watch over my father all night for five nights, sitting next to his bed with a stack of murder mysteries at our feet. Every hour or so my father would wake, rise as if it were morning and spot some speck on the floor that deserved close inspection. He would lean to pick it up, and I or my mother would jump to attention. "Daddy! Don't! Do you want to go blind?!" And he, his face crumpled with hurt and confusion, turned to me and asked: "Amy. Why are you yelling at your father?" I don't know, I don't know.

It's been hard to let go of my old father, to bid farewell to his gentle, shuffling presence here on earth. I loved him as he was. Yet as I say good-bye, I am struck by the emergence of another father, the one whose books line my wall, whose long career echoes in every whisper of my own. How often I stumble across something he wrote -- on a record jacket, a program, in a magazine or (once) on the Web -- and wonder at his facility with words. Though his old age passed with death, his youth remains in his work. I read it and hear my father, full, alive, singing with confidence and vigor.

The man in the photo waits on my shelf, laughing. I search his face and find there not the ghost of a person I never knew but the birth of someone new, someone whose strength and humor carry me through my grief. He offers a hand of friendship, and I grasp.

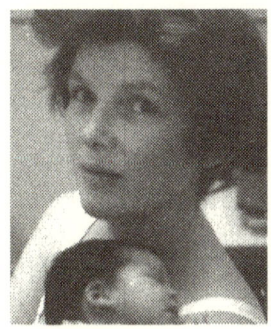

5

What a Dame

She died planting a tree. That's not strictly true but it's lovely to say so, because even if she didn't quite, she should have; I could have cooked up no more fitting way for my mother to make her exit. Always nurturing, always pruning bushes or sweet-talking rows of day lilies, she had a green thumb and an intrepid and crusty nature that prohibited her from ever giving up on any plant. The thing could be brown and curled at the edges, and she'd find some way to revive it. "Maybe a little water and a move to the landing will wake it up," she'd say, watering it and moving it to the landing, where it would wake up.

She died planting a tree. It was a bronze maple sapling, a housewarming gift for me and my husband; we had moved into our new home eight months earlier, when I was ludicrously pregnant (full term and counting) with Madeleine. She waited until spring to plant it. She'd arrived for a visit the evening before, the sapling stooped uncomfortably in the back of her bulbous three-cylinder car, her violin riding on the floor in the back. She came in, hugged me, hugged Chris, told us about the maple, told us she'd pick a spot for it the following morning, told us we'd have to water it and water it and water it, then asked me if I still wanted her to come along to that chamber-music rehearsal I'd told her about. I said of course. She said, Are you sure? I said, Only if you want to, Mama. She said, Golly of course I'd love to if you'll have me but I don't want to intrude, you know. I said, Mama don't be a nerd I love to play with you, come along. So she came along.

We drove with Karl, my violist friend, over to a nearby college where Linda, another violist friend, conducted an amateur summer chamber orchestra. The rehearsal took place in a small pale room, and there were many young women with long hair and brightly varnished instruments. Some of them stared at Mama while she warmed up; most amateurs don't whip off double-stop arpeggios in fifth position just to get their fingers wagging. But Mama insisted on playing second violin with me (little me, fallible me, born to play second), so she sat at my left, sharing my stand. For two and a half hours we played Boccherini or Arriaga or some such else. At evening's close we drove Karl home, then stopped at a sandwich shop to pick up subs. We ate them in the kitchen, Mama and I, while Chris tried to pry Mama off the blue plastic milk crate she was sitting on and get her into a normal chair. She didn't want to: She preferred to suffer. Oh I'm Fine Sleeping on Shards of Glass, Don't Worry About Me, I Like Being Uncomfortable, I'm Just a Hair Shirt In Human Form. We watched a few minutes of television and went off to bed. She slept on the couch. Around 8 a.m. the next morning she dressed, headed out the front door and started digging a hole for the sapling.

That's when I had the dream. You know how vivid morning dreams are: The colors are overexposed, like those laminated landscapes in a dentist's office, the ones that are supposed to calm us down but in reality lead us to suspect that the dentist is actually Sir Laurence Olivier in the torture scene from "Marathon Man." Olivier did not

figure in my dream that morning, but William Shatner did.
I don't know why, and am in fact somewhat embarrassed
to admit it. I refuse to believe it stems from my crush on
him at age 13, because I had crushes on several other
characters at age 13, and none of them appeared in a
psychic dream on the morning of my mother's death
(Brian Strandes, are you out there?). Of course, my mother
had confessed to me that she, too, once had a crush on
William Shatner – when he was on Broadway and live TV,
I think. So perhaps that's why. Or perhaps I have an
extrasensory link with Captain Kirk. Or perhaps it's best
not to dwell on this too much.

In any case, I dreamed that Mama was performing
for a small group of people, me included. Shatner sat next
to me. As she played, I gave him a blow-by-blow account
of her career -- all of the praise she'd earned, all of the
world tours she'd done, all of the times she played
Carnegie and soloed with the Philly. My spiel was
interrupted when Mama collapsed, mid-piece. I knew at
once she was dying: "Mama don't go," I said. "Mama
don't go, Mama don't go, don't go, Mama, Mama don't
go." I cradled her head in my arms and realized with
horror that her eyes, while open, did not see me. Then she
retreated behind a row of bars, and was gone.

I awoke and told Chris immediately. "It's just a
dream," he said. "Your mother's going to live forever."
And as the young sun coursed through our windows, I
heard Mama outside, digging her hole, and felt relieved.
She was still alive.

Half an hour later I was out there with the baby,
helping Mama hack away roots from a nearby Norway.
While digging she told me that earlier in the morning she'd
lost her balance and smacked her head on the sidewalk.
When? I asked. Oh, not long ago, she said. You okay? I
asked. Sure, sure, she said. Got a whopper of a headache.
That older gentleman down the street, the elegant black
man, he helped me up. Nice man, she said. Oh, I said.

Around 9 o'clock Mama drove to the hardware

store for an extra length of garden hose -- to water the tree after planting. Around 10 o'clock she came back. Around 10:30 she started vomiting. You okay? I asked. Oh, probably a concussion, she said. From when I fell. I'll take you to the hospital, I said. You'll Do No Such Thing, she said, and puked again. I'd better sit down, she said.

She sat down. She looked awful – sweaty, pink in the face, empty. I said I was going to phone her doctor in Connecticut. She didn't argue.

Her doctor in Connecticut told me to phone an ambulance immediately: She's on blood thinners for her strokes, he reminded me. If she's bleeding. . . .

I phoned 911. The fire department answered, switched me to the ambulance, which took forever – a minute or two – to answer. While waiting for a response I cried. "Don't die, Mama, Don't die, Mama. Mama don't die,'' I said, and thought of my dream.

After reaching the EMTs I walked back to the love seat where Mama sat, sweating. Her eyes were half-open, unfocused, dim. She didn't see me. She was comatose by then. I spoke to her, told her an ambulance was coming, told her I loved her, told her she'd been a great mother, told her I couldn't have asked for anything more from a parent.

I phoned Chris and told him Mama was dying. "Honey, you don't know that,'' he said. She is, I said. She's dying. I know it.

He came while the EMTs were strapping her down. One, a woman, asked me what medications Mama had been on, but I couldn't remember. I couldn't find her medicine bag. So I phoned Mama's doctor and handed the receiver to the EMT.

Chris rode in the ambulance with Mama. I followed in a car with Madeleine; I wouldn't leave my baby, wouldn't put her in a careening ambulance without a proper child seat. Once in the emergency room I reunited with Chris, then waited. They're giving her a CT scan, he said.

Twenty minutes later a neurosurgeon came in, took us to a small, closed side room off the main waiting area and told us a subdural hematoma had washed out a piece of Mama's brain. Subdural hematoma: a swelling of blood in the head. Thanks to her blood thinners, it was getting bigger by the second. If we wanted him to operate, we'd have to say so immediately. Did we want him to operate?

We said: What are her chances? Would surgery help?

He said: I don't know. She might live for a few more days. And then maybe she'd die anyway. Or maybe surgery would be successful. But a hematoma this big --

We said: Would she recover?

He said: I don't know. A hematoma this big –

We said: She's a violinist. She's supposed to play the Glazunov Concerto next spring.

He said: Well.

We said: Can we have a minute?

He said: A minute. I'll be back in a minute.

Chris and I looked at each other. It was easy. Not a month earlier, Mama had told me not to take "hysterical measures" if she were ever seriously ill. She filled out a will and a health-care proxy. She sat me down and told me she "had her ticket" and was ready for the next world whenever God said so. In those words. She said she felt confident I'd be fine without her, said she was proud of me and knew my life was on track and bound to be rich in love. She said she looked forward to seeing Daddy and Lucy again. Said she was at peace, at ease, not afraid of death at all. I should not fear losing her, she said. I would be okay. She said so. She promised.

I knew what Mama wanted: She wanted us to let her die. When the neurosurgeon returned he glanced at us in a way that said, Well? And we said, No, don't operate. If we told you to operate it would be for us, not for her. For her we should do nothing. For her we should step aside and let her die, just let her die, just let. And he nodded and said, That's very wise.

Later on another doctor said the same thing: That's very wise. That's very wise.

I don't know if it was wise; maybe it was rash, driven not by reason but by love. Or maybe wisdom is rash. Maybe it isn't reasonable at all.

We asked the neurosurgeon how long a wait we had. He said six to eight hours. It was noon; she died at 8 p.m. In the last hours of her life I sat with her, stroked her brow as she once stroked mine, held her left hand – small, square, of plain utilitarian beauty, its fingers calloused from years of playing the fiddle. I talked to her through the rail on her bed (the bars from my dream): I told her again and again that it was okay to go, that I loved her and knew she'd be happy where she's headed. Madeleine was with us, so I nursed her and played with her and lay her down to nap on Mama's bed, between her legs. After a while I asked Chris to go home and get the violin; I wanted to play for my mother.

He brought back Mama's violin, made for her in the sixties by a luthier named Karl August Berger, and I played it. Mama, I said. Mama, I have your violin. I'm going to play Fritz Kreisler for you, Mama. "Liebesleid.'' (A piece I never could get right; Mama was always after me to nail the rhythms.) Mama, I'll try to play it correctly, I said, but I might mess up. I'm sorry if I mess up. But I'm going to play it now. Here I go, Mama.

So I played it. I messed it up. But I played it with love, I played it knowing it was the last music Mama would hear on Earth, I played it hoping she would hear not my errors but my simple goodbye behind them. And when I finished playing, I looked at her, and saw that a tear had streaked her face.

I never realized how hesitant, how gradual, death can be. In movies and on television shows people always expire suddenly: Heart attack! Bam! Pow! Insta-Dead! My mother-in-law's departure was swift and clear. But in

Mama's case it was much less discrete. Her heartbeat weakened. Her breaths became less frequent – first every few seconds, then every minute, then every few minutes, then once every five or ten. In the final ninety minutes or so Chris and I would check the hummingbird flutter of her pulse, figure how long it'd been since the last breath, and ask: Is she dead now? Is a woman dead who hasn't breathed in fifteen minutes and whose heart couldn't pump blood through a fly? Who knew whether she was brain dead at that point; I had no idea. We spent Mama's closing hour trying to decide if she was still alive.

A handful of friends were with us. Early on Chris had phoned the newspaper where we both worked and said, Amy's Mom is dying in Albany Med. If anyone wants to come, thank you.

Several people came. And of the several who came, four or five stayed until the final reckoning. When twenty minutes had passed since Mama's last breath and we couldn't see the pulse in her neck any longer, I said, "I guess she's dead," then cried and held her hand and kissed her. Chris said, "Oh, Jeanne."

One of our friends dropped to his knees and prayed. Everyone else was quiet. I rubbed the calluses on her fingertips; the pad on her index finger was thickest. I thought: After today, I'll never hold this hand again. I must never forget how it feels to touch these calluses. I must never forget the soft shiny back to her hand, or the coolness of it, or the feeling of the bones beneath her skin. Remembering her hand meant remembering the music that she made with it and the life that came with the music. I knew that, I was sure of it, it terrified me. So far, I haven't forgotten.

*****

Let me tell you about my mother. She was a wacky lady. She was a smart lady. She was a lady who said anything that was on her mind, at any moment, regardless of the potential outcome. She was a lady who got into many car accidents, then denied it had anything to do with her driving (The Deer Are Everywhere This Time of Year). She was an angry lady who learned to make sense of her temper and decided to let it go. She was a reading lady, a crossword-puzzling lady, a Scrabbling lady, a crytpogrammatical lady and the kind of lady who looked at a "Men At Work" sign and said, aloud, "NEM TA KROW! She was a lady who liked to hammer and saw. She was a wiry lady, with ropy arms and neck muscles that took four interns to yank apart before surgeons could get at her thyroid (Is that true, Mama?). She was a lady of voluminous arcane knowledge. She was a lovely lady, a lifelong beauty with sky-blue eyes and ash-colored hair that turned cloud white. She was a lady who took no bull from anyone. She said what she liked. She ate what she liked, as long as salt wasn't involved. She loved cats. She hated dogs. She loved plants. She hated cold. She was tough. Sharp. Loving. Scary. Indestructible.

She knew music. She heard the chords in every car horn, knew intuitively where to take a phrase, pulled pitches out of thin air with breezy accuracy. ("Hey, Jeanne, give me an E,'' said Daddy, meaning the vitamin. She gave him the note.) She could play the violin as though it were her other self. She could stand on a stage and mesmerize everyone who sat before her, then put away her fiddle and say outrageous funny honest things while eating gummi worms and strings of black licorice in front of the tube. She could cut her hair short as a toothbrush and wear no more make-up than a thin swipe of lipstick, and still she'd be the only person anyone was watching in a room. She had charisma. She had confidence. She had no false modesty whatsoever. But she was truly, profoundly, and I am not pulling your leg on this, humble.

It came from knowing God. Even before Mama knew she knew God, she knew God – she knew, in other words, that something outside of her (a something else, a somewhere else) had given her the gift to make music.

Probably it had to do with DNA, parents, grandparents and the fruitful chaos of nature's carom with upbringing. She simply understood that her ability to perform – ultimately, her ability to communicate, the power of all great artists – was not something she alone could take credit for. In this way she was humble. Yet she saw no point in denying or downplaying her gifts; she saw no point in being modest about something that wasn't entirely hers. Why would she? If someone had said, "Jeanne, the sky is azure today," she wouldn't have responded: "No, no, you're too kind, it's much too drab to be called 'azure.' " When someone told her, "Jeanne, your playing lifts and inspires me and shows me the beauty of Bach," she didn't deny it. Instead she said, "Thank you." And if her arthritis was acting up that day, she said, "I'm grateful these old hands still let me play."

They let her play, all right. As lax as she was about housecleaning, she was meticulous with the violin. She knew how to work: methodically, addressing the most difficult sections first, over and over, figuring the fingerings, figuring the phrases, figuring the dynamics, figuring the musical bends around a piece. She had an infallible instincts, tremendous poise and rugged power: Onstage she formed a knotty plug of talent and determination. Her cheeks reddened. Her brow turned damp. The sinew in her arms creased and popped. But her left hand, that broad little calloused little hand, barely moved; it picked out the melody with economy and grace, never leaping off the fingerboard, never indulging in gymnastic feats that had nothing to do with music. Pyrotechnics for the sake of pyrotechnics bored her. He's playing too fast, she'd say of a colleague. He's forgetting what he's there for. He's forgetting the music.

Say what you will about my old dead fiddler of a ma, but not once in her life did she forget the music.

*****

Jeanne Frances Mitchell was born in Wilmington, North Carolina, four years behind her brother, Alexander – Allie Boy, they called him. Her father, Joseph Scott Mitchell, was a proud autodidact who worshipped the written word and had taught himself sufficient law to pass the bar. He had piles of auburn hair, a dead man's grip and a gaze that could pierce stone. Jeanne's mother, Hazel Madeleine Langenberg Mitchell, was a powerful woman from a long line of powerful women with gifts for teaching and music. She played viola. Allie played piano, later viola. Joe played nothing, although he could hear entire symphonies in his head and Mama swore he was the most naturally musical member of her family. Mama took piano and violin lessons, eventually focusing on the violin; her first and last teacher was a ferocious tiny man named Chester LaFollette, a nephew of "Fighting Bob" LaFollette, the legendary Congressman from Wisconsin. (Chester, a gifted artist, painted a portrait of his uncle that hangs in the Senate reception room.) Whenever Mama told stories about her childhood her vowels slipped, her consonants turned to mush and single-syllable words became scooping Carolina diphthongs. On the phone with her brother she let loose Al-lays and Hun-nays and Maw-mas and How ye' doins', none of which I ever heard her use in normal conversation. Most of the time (barring those occasions when her musician's ear forced her to mimic whomever she was with), she talked like a Yank. But in her bones, in her childhood, she was a southerner.

In fact, she spent very few years below the Mason-Dixon line. While she was still a toddler her family left North Carolina for Florida (where her Daddy was bilked in a real-estate deal), and a few years after that to Floral Park, Long Island, where she blossomed from a knock-kneed twig of a girl into a slim blonde beauty. They were poor – Great Depression poor, which means they were deprived of their money but not their backbone, not their assiduity or pluck. The bankers who pitched from window ledges didn't know enough to live; they didn't know, as did

Mama's family, as did all leather-souled survivors of the era, that courage and acceptance are the same thing. Not complacency – not despair. Acceptance. Accept your lot, and do what you have to do you reach tomorrow. I must have heard a thousand times my mother's story of the gray-skied afternoon when her Daddy shimmied up a smokestack with a plumb line in his teeth. He did it for a dollar. Horrified as she was, she didn't doubt the need that sent him up there. She didn't hate her father for the fear (hers) or the risk (his). Poverty meant living with imperatives: He had to go up. She had to accept that he had to go up. Up he went.

That was Mama's greatest strength, I think – her willingness to take her life on its own screwy terms. No matter the rubbish that came her way, she worked with it, figured out a way to turn it into something a bit less noxious for her and all. She knew how to savor things -- the bite of lemon sucked through a stick of sugar cane, the thrill of getting lost on a midnight car trip. "We'll have an adventure, girls," she'd say, peering over the wheel of her Corolla, her thin lips cracking toward a grin. Far from unrufflable (Mama, why'd you throw that chair across the floor? Why'd you toss the salad bowl instead of just the salad?), her temper flared in hypertensive bursts and then cooled to a state of relaxed, self-deprecatory goofiness. Even her anger had an upside -- she was easy to make up with, funny for hours afterward. I didn't know her as a child but imagine her as a flinty devil, hard and smart and quick on the uptake. A survivor. A doer. A coper -- is that a word? One who copes. When my father's last good teeth rotted out and he refused to get dentures, Mama had all of her own teeth pulled -- the good along with the bad -- to persuade him to follow suit, knowing her queerly intractable husband wouldn't go through with it unless she did first. She did what she had to do.

(On the subject of dentures: She was cleaning them one day when she lost her grip and lurched forward to catch them before they dropped, accidentally propelling them, and I swear this is true, into a mouse hole. Presumably they're still there. In an unrelated incident, she once used this same technique to throw a frozen chicken at Peter the cat, who thereafter crossed the kitchen like a grunt dodging hand grenades.)

"She's a tough old nut," Mama liked to say of whatever old lady she admired, and that's what she became: a tough old nut. She'd been one all of her life. When I confessed to her my curious fantasy of being very young and very old, but never my true age, she confessed the same. "You have that, too? I've had that since I was a kid," she said, and shook her head. So much alike, we two. What separated us beyond 40 years was the drive to perform. Mama had it. Lucy had it. I didn't, don't. I enjoy being the center of attention but don't need it and don't note its absence. Mama needed it. She couldn't stop playing, ever; on doctor's orders she retired from performing in her 60s after the second of three small strokes, but it didn't stick. Within two or three years of her "retirement" she was at it again, first as concert master for the Ridgefield (Connecticut) Symphony Orchestra, then as a soloist in the Brahms Double Concerto. A season or two later she'd signed on to solo again, this time with the Glazunov. She practiced like mad; now and then she'd ring up and play a passage for me over the phone, proud of the music still in her. "I'm playing better than I ever did. This Glazunov's gonna be something," she said.

I haven't heard it since she died. Not a recording, not a live performance, not a few measures' snip on the radio. I can't bring myself to listen, preferring instead the imagined thrill of my mother's promised Glazunov.

*****

Mama's public debut took place in her eighth or ninth year, at a joint recital of Chester's pupils. This was after Hazel and Allie and Jeanne and Joe moved north; Jeanne and Allie studied violin and piano, respectively, from Chester and his wife, respectively, who ran a bustling music school in Manhattan. Jeanne had previously only played the violin facing her teacher, who sat at the piano and accompanied, so that's how she stood to perform -- with her back to the audience. Chester had to turn the little girl around. (I love that story: It reminds me of Beethoven, by then stone deaf, being turned around to see the ovation following the premiere of his Ninth Symphony.) Mama was filial in her love for the LaFollettes and remained under Chester's tutelage through her entire career. He was her only teacher -- she never felt compelled to trade him in for a more widely celebrated (or influential, or connected) instructor. Mama was never politically shrewd, not in that way; otherwise she might have accepted Jascha Heifetz's offer to teach her, an opportunity she turned down after an arranged meeting with the virtuoso left her less than wowed. She played a Schubert sonata and Prokofiev's Concerto in G minor, one of Heifetz's signature pieces. When Heifetz proferred no comment beyond a few bored queries about her fingering, Mama thought: Forget this. There's nothing to learn here. I guess I'll stick with Chester.

At the LaFollettes' school she befriended the American pianist William Kapell, who found world fame by 20 and died in a plane crash at 31. She remembered him as driven, charismatic, electric; he entered a room, and the bolts would fly. ("Willy Kapell had a fire lit under him.") She also met Bess Myerson, whom New Yorkers know as Ed Koch's scandal-magnet girlfriend. Willy Kapell could never understand why Bess, not Jeanne, won the 1945 Miss America pageant. "Jeanne should've won it," he said -- rather, Mama said he said, adding by way of clarification that Willy Kapell was a Gorgeous Young Man and Oooh-Whoo, Did He Make Your Hair Stand On End When He Looked At You. (Incidentally, did she mention the time a single-prop plane she was in tipped its wing in choppy waters and nearly crashed and she saw the hair on the guy in front of her *shoot straight up*? And that the handsomest man she ever saw held her head while she puked? And while we're on the subject of planes, did she ever tell you about the time she was on tour in Spain and she was in this teensy-weensy airport in this teensy-weensy town and she was looking for her Connecting Flight and she couldn't find it, anywhere, and she couldn't find a single person or moving vehicle, anywhere, until she finally found this little guy with a mop and a bucket and even though she couldn't speak Spanish she managed to ask the guy where her Connecting Flight was and when he finally understood her he said, "Oh. . . thee plane. . . ees broke"? And while we're on the subject of funny accents, did she ever tell you about her manager overseas, who had this thick Eastern European accent and spoke really really bad English and was once propositioned by a Loose Woman but didn't know her history and later confessed to Mama that he "deed not know her SAX-uall behind"?)

Mama loved Chester, she loved the school, she loved to talk about those days. When Chris and I first started dating we were stunned to realize that his father, Eugene Ringwald, took lessons from Chester, too -- but didn't have nearly so fond a memory of him. Eugene couldn't remember his name -- ". . . was it Chip Lefever? Chuck Levalle?" -- but recalled a short, thorny character who held sway over a Manhattan music school. He also recalled being told brusquely to quit the violin as he was wasting his parents' money. When Mama heard this she confirmed the I.D. -- "yes, that's Chester" -- and gave the bluntness a shrug. She liked blunt people. At least she knew where she was with them.

Young Jeanne grew, finished up high school (Horace Mann), went to Barnard. Became BWOC without evening trying. Hung out with artists and swells in equal measure. Piled into an old Stanley Steamer, rode around town shoveling coal and laughing. Played music, read philosophy, dated -- though not seriously, I gathered. Mostly guys got crushes on her. It was the war years, and girls had eyes for uniforms. Once a shipload of sailors docked in for a campus dance, and the Barnard gals all tossed their left shoes into a pile. Each sailor picked out a shoe and his date for the evening: Mama got matched with her cousin George, a sailor on the ship in question, whom she was always pleased to see but not right then, not right there. But the gangly beauty had fun that evening, dancing with her cousin, smiling her ruddy generous smile, saying what she thought without the brakes on. Most people flirt via falsehoods, however minor, however twee, but not Mama. She wooed the world with honesty.

That helped her, I think, in the years that followed. Only the unsentimental can face tragedy and success with equal clarity and ease; most of us handle one better the other, or neither well at all. Post-Barnard life unfolded neatly for Jeanne: a job as a section player in Leopold Stokowski's New York City Symphony came first, yielding a lifetime's worth of affectionate "Stokey" stories. (When Stokey was looking for an assistant, Mama gave him the name of her roommate. He phoned; the roommate answered; he announced, "Hello, this is Leopold Stokowski"; she snapped, "And I'm Arturo Toscanini!" and hung up. She got the job.) One day during rehearsal she told a few colleagues that she was leaving to embark on a solo career, but not everyone was happy for her. "Some of them could play rings around me," she used to say, meaning: She wasn't the best, but she had the nerve. And you need nerve to take that leap into the spotlight.

On Tuesday, December 9, 1947 she made her New York City debut in Town Hall. In 1949 The New York Times announced: "The name of Jeanne Mitchell. . . is one that belongs near the head of the list of up-and-coming young violinists. Great violinists who have already arrived have arrived without anything nearly so stunning in their repertory as her performance of Prokofiev's G-Minor." ("A born fiddler, whose birthmark is on every phrase she plays. . . one of the best brains in music today," wrote some guy named Biancolli.) By 1957 she had performed six solo recitals in Carnegie Hall. She went on three world tours. She soloed with the New York Philharmonic, the Hague Symphony, the St. Louis Symphony and the Philadelphia Orchestra. Most significantly, she found a mentor and cheerleader in Eugene Ormandy, who hired her to solo with the Philly half a dozen times and regarded her as one of the bright young lights of the violin. (Ormandy was so close to my parents that when I was born in 1963 he gave them a silver baby cup engraved with my initials and his looping signature.) By the time she married Daddy in 1958 at the age of 35, she had already achieved most of her professional goals and was well on her way toward achieving the rest.

Then something happened. Maybe it was fate in a spiteful mood, maybe God in a snit, but the Dutch label that had just recorded her debut album folded without warning before its release. Before it was even *pressed* -- she never learned what happened to the tapes. Her concert career cooled as her personal life assumed top priority: marriage to an unstable man, then motherhood. Step by step she pulled back from performing, never "retiring," exactly, but devoting more and more time to two small girls and their loving but cockeyed father. She always thought she'd return to global concertizing. By the time she felt ready to -- when Lucy and I were both in school, maybe 5 and 8 -- she approached her former mentor and told him she was poised for a return. She asked Ormandy for a chance to solo with the Philly once more. He said (politely, I expect), No. He implied there was only room for one female violinist, and since she'd left to have kids, another had entered stage right. He said: You chose to leave. I can't help you. Sorry.

I have to hand it to my mother: She was never bitter. At least, she never seemed bitter to me -- Lucy and I never felt the blame for ruining her career, though surely we were a major cause. She didn't even tell us about Ormandy's role until we were in our 20s. Mama accepted her lot, and she loved us; she didn't regret motherhood. The

violin was always there, always a part of who she was, and
she kept right on playing in churches and school halls and
small-town arts centers in and around western Connecticut.

Long before it was fashionable, Mama postponed
marriage and motherhood to have a career. "I was an
elderly primipara," she'd boast, using the then-voguish
medical term for an older first-time mother -- 37 when
Lucy was born. "I never felt like a trailblazer," she'd say. "I
never tried to make some kind of statement. I just had my
career. And when it was time to fall in love and have kids,
I did." She was amused by the 1970s' most ardent
feminists, who made big noises about parity but (she felt)
often missed the point on the larger issues of home and
family. She also found them a bit ridiculous in their
extremism -- burning bras ("It's more *comfortable* to wear
a bra"), lying down in city streets ("You don't win anyone
to your side"), shrieking into microphones at fresh-air
rallies ("Women with high voices should never yell"),
placing misguided emphasis on picayune word choice and
awkwardly de-sexed language. "I'll Ms. anyone if she
prefers it," she wrote in a hilarious rant to Barnard
Alumnae magazine (Summer 1974, letters page). "But call
me anything you like, just not too early." She went on in
vociferously good humor about men and women for
several long paragraphs. The full diatribe is repeated
below.

> I sleep late -- until 5:30. Then I get up, put
> on something frilly and ruffly like blue jeans and
> make breakfast for the beautiful children of my
> middle years. After they're on the school bus I
> languidly neglect the house and practice the violin
> hard for a while, to seduce my man -- which is an
> old object-female maneuver recommended in
> Godey's Lady's Book -- and it always makes him
> close his door and type with earplugs in. Then I fix
> lunch because otherwise Tums and to be
> magnanimous I let him have any scraps that are

left. After which I leave to tape an interview or coach chamber music for hours or counsel students, just in order to make him wild with possessiveness. It's a good gambit because he can't wait for me to leave so he can remove the earplugs and bang out Scott Joplin on the piano. It really takes ruthless talent to be a kept woman.

2) What's to be done with concertmaster-concertmistress? Concertperson? That's nondescriptive. Of course, "concertmistress" isn't helpful either if she's single and wants us to be sure about it. But then "chairman" itself is hilarious. It meant something once, when big-shots sat in big chairs while all the serfs stood around on legs like logs wishing they could scratch the soles of their feet. Only the odd ruling queen was big-shotty enough to have the biggest chair of all, and I bet she didn't care too much about male domination. I bet she was more concerned with that chair. (Now, the serf's wife: aha!). . . ConcertMASTRESS? Think of what a tired typesetter could do with that. My keeper the etymologist ("husband": dweller in the house) told me that he never again used the word "recital" in his newspaper column after it once appeared in an early edition with the one crucial letter missing. So I told him about a review I got once which still unsettles me unless I fight hard. It said I "presented a violent concert last night." I'm ashamed to show it to my children. (Could it have been phoned in to the copy desk and dictated to a nonspeller?)

You may take out the earplugs now, I'm through.

Feminist or no, Mama belonged to the League of Women Voters. She also belonged to the League of Staunch Individualists, the League of Smart Broads and the League of Fed-Up Women in an Age of Widespread

Male Stupidity. She stuck up for herself in the face of sexism and felt residual frustration with every dorkhead music critic (Daddy included) who couldn't get past the fact that she was a gorgeous blonde. There was invariably an "I must add. . . " clause in every review, a sentence or two in which Miss Mitchell was revealed as quite the hubba-hubba specimen. (To be fair, the most egregious instance of this occurred in the New York Post by the female critic Harriett Johnson, who declared, "The cliché 'beautiful but dumb' will never be applied to Jeanne Mitchell.") This drove her to distraction, and it drove her (I think) to de-emphasize the whole make-up and fashion business with me and Lucy. Glamour was never one of her goals.

She taught us to be tough cookies. One day I told Mama about some chest-beaters on the playground who boasted "IT'S A MAN'S WORLD" while teetering on a see-saw. Mama's response was immediate. "Tell them they're wrong," she said. "Tell them it's not a man's world. It's a woman's world. Tell them that." I did as instructed, and those poor boys -- they looked confused. If they'd been characters in a comic book, question marks would have popped over their heads like a cloud of gnats. Growing up female in the '70s meant being acutely, politically aware of one's place (or not) in the pernicious male schema -- there was even a television ad that characterized American females as handicapped from birth. But my mother, bless her testy old soul, managed to give us pride in our girlhood without demonizing the opposite sex or making us feel like victims. She stressed education ("You'll have to live with your head for the rest of your life, so you'd better make it interesting"). She stressed independence. She gave us the strength to fight peer pressure, then trusted us when we were alone. She counseled us against making stupid choices, and most of the time, we didn't. I never experimented with drugs or sex, and thanks to Mama's encyclopedic reproductive instruction (Say, that's a nice fallopian tube you've drawn there!), I knew more about the

birds and the bees than any girl I knew. I'd never seen an
erect penis, but I knew why my friend's beau had to race
from the room after necking with her ("So that's why. . . "
she said, eyes widening with comprehension).

I admired and enjoyed my mom, even when I
found her impossible. We fought sometimes, particularly
during my teenage years. But I saw in her a model of self-
reliance cut with altruism that sticks with me to this day:
She was true to herself, but not in an architect-meets-
dynamite kind of way; she wasn't Gary Cooper
demolishing a compromised skyscraper in the Ayn Rand
heroics of "The Fountainhead." She was true to herself by
giving expression to her most generous impulses -- by
being honest and self-sacrificing, by sticking to her
marriage vows once her husband had lost his mind. This
humanity informed her music, lent it passion and
compassion and a prismal edge. Her every word and action
bespoke a ruthless candor tempered by love. That's who
she was. That's why she remained, dashed global career
notwithstanding, one of the greatest concert violinists this
country ever produced. I'm her daughter. I lack
perspective. On the subject of my mother I'm completely,
impossibly, laughably, wholeheartedly biased. But I'm
right.

We read about history's major figures, about
people who set goals and achieve them thanks to a
fortuitous mix of talent, ambition and timing. Dumb luck
helps. But luck can turn the other way, ambition can take a
back seat to necessity, and talent can express itself in more
modestly scaled arenas. This I learned from my mother's
life and career: That great art retains its greatness even as
its audience shrinks or turns its attention elsewhere. As
tragedy and the humdrum chores of life peeled back the
artifice from her art, Mama's music grew more resonant
and enriched. By the end of her life she was playing better
than ever, arthritis be damned; one of the things I've
missed most in the years since her death is hearing her
perform live. I miss hugging her backstage at intermission

and feeling her moist pink cheek against my own. Most of all, I miss seeing the expressions on people's faces, the awakened demi-smile of gratitude and surprise that marks a collision with beauty. "Thank you," they would say, reaching hesitantly for her hand in a crowded green room. Always thank you: Thank you for sharing with us. Thank you for a Beautiful Evening. Thank you for coming to play here tonight. Thank you for that magnificent music. Magnificent violin. Magnificent vibrato. Magnificent tone. Magnificent Magnificence Magnified Magnificently by a Magnificent Musician. Thank you.

In reply, Mama always said: You're welcome. Thank you for coming. Did you like the Franck? That's some piece, huh?

That's some piece, Mama. That's some gal playing it. As Daddy liked to say, What a Dame. Oh, My Jeannie. What a Dame.

*****

Five or six years after Daddy quit the World-Telegram, things got tight in the house on the lake. I don't remember how tight, or how this manifested itself in our day-to-day operations (were our faces smeared with jam?), or even if it did. But I do know that Mama felt compelled to get a job. This compulsion led her to Wykeham Rise, that small girls' arts school, where she became a music teacher (eventually head of the department) and my family's chief provider. Daddy couldn't or wouldn't provide, so she did. She was a pragmatist and an egghead; indeed, pragmatism cleared the path toward enlightenment with the bushwhacking force of a woodsman. She always saw clearly what was needed of her, and she always responded as asked.

Wykeham was an unusual place. I say "was"; it no longer exists. The buildings are still there – gracious Colonials flanked by concrete dorms, which later spent a summer hosting the Rolling Stones and eventually morphed into a hospitality school – but the life of the place was snuffed out long ago by financial pressures. Lucy and I both attended: Lucy for four years of intensive piano study, I for three years of this and that and the other thing (voice, soccer, ceramics -- those pinch pots). I made lasting friendships there with Wykeham's headmaster, a bighearted paterfamilias we called Boss, and his wife and three kids. (They've since become my surrogate family; after Mama's death, their eldest son wrote to tell me, "Consider my parents yours.")

Wykeham was affectionate, informal, small. It was rich in people, rich in art. It was a second home for us all. More than a home, it was a kitchen, the place in a house where soups get made and people in pajamas share their dreams and nightmares. Kids came from all backgrounds. There were Juilliard-trained aesthetes, pre-professional theater geeks, scrappy characters from the inner city, poised, slim dancers, girls with troubled histories, jingly retro-hippies, blacks, whites, Latinas, Asians, even someone who'd had an out-of-body experience. Classes were eight kids, six kids, sometimes one or two. Everyone knew everyone. Teachers were Willie and Doc and Meals and Fletch. The cook was Winnie; she doubled as disciplinarian and chief confessor, a woman whose icy glare could spot a lie a mile off. Artists came for semester-long residencies and left amazed at the school's idiosyncrasy and warmth: the dancer Bill T. Jones, the pianist Leon Bates. "Did you think Wykeham was a special place?" a friend asked me, years after its collapse. In reply I could only stare at him -- was that a serious question? "Yeah," I finally managed, and that was that.

Wykeham did something none of us expected at the time: It introduced us to the structures of religion. The first church I sat in and sang in as a willing participant was an Episcopal church of cool gray stone where Wykeham girls matriculated in boxy red jackets. The first church Mama attended on a regular basis was that same, small

congregation, led by a booming Armenian-American
pastor with an expansive personality and a mind like a
trap. Eventually she started playing organ there. Eventually
Lucy and I tagged along and slipped inconspicuously into
the pews, where we belted out thrumming minor-key
hymns rife with the battle-calls of faith.

> Once to ev'ry man and nation
> 　　comes the moment to decide
> In the strife of truth with falsehood
> 　　for the good or evil side
> One great cause, God's new Messiah,
> 　　off'ring each of bloom or blight
> And the choice goes by forever
> 　　'twixt that darkness and that light.

****

Mega-zoom on the year 1974. The merry Biancolli
clan embark on a cruise through the Caribbean. It's not
their first vacation -- they once spent a week or two in a
cottage on Long Island Sound -- but it's far and away their
one big splurge. The whole thing must cost thousands. But
Jeanne has demanded it of Louis: she feels her family
needs it, she feels the kids need it, she feels she needs it.
Somehow she persuades him on all three points, though
their children are never sure how; perhaps she threatens to
cut off his supply of Wheat Germ.

They purchase polyester summer clothes in garish
colors. They fly to Miami and take an airport shuttle to the
Federico C., an elegant cruiseliner staffed by strapping
Southern Italians in starched white uniforms. They all
speak Neapolitan. Once the Biancollis arrive, they all
speak Neapolitan to Louis -- to the girls it sounds like
music, with its mellifluous phrasings and glissando runs of
syllables. Louis looks happy. Jeanne looks happy watching
him -- his arms are wide, his smile is wide, his chest is
wide and brown. The girls sun themselves and eat frogs'

legs and rum cake and swim in kidney-shaped pools with
gawky rich kids. They play shuffleboard in a shipboard
tournament; Amy practices, Lucy wins. They ogle the
ship's crew, particularly a hunk named Dino whose biceps
hold them in thrall. Their mother does nothing but sit and
read until Gigi, the wiry first mate, reveals himself as an
amateur luthier and asks her to perform. On one of his
gawdawful violins. On the second-to-last day of the cruise.

Jeanne says yes, not because she wants to say yes,
but because she can't say no: She never says no, not when
someone asks her to play. She once played for a stranger in
Central Park. So she practices. Day after day, hour after
hour, she practices, spending the bulk of her cruise through
paradise in a cabin, practicing the violin.

The ship stops in Jamaica, St. Thomas, Puerto
Rico. In Jamaica a large-muscled man named Tiny lifts the
girls onto the back of a burro. In St. Thomas they swim in
a sea of lucent blues and greens, and Jeanne falls in love
with a Flamboyant Tree. In Puerto Rico she buys a music
box with a peasant child playing the fiddle.

The ship swings northward. Jeanne gives her
concert: a bit of Kreisler, a bit of Bach. Louis and the girls
are very proud. On the last day of the cruise Jeanne begins
to cough. And they go home.

Back in New Preston the girls show off their tans,
and Jeanne's cough worsens. At first she figures it's just a
smoker's hack -- she's been three-packs-a-day since her
twenties. Then she thinks it's a holdover from the ship's
faulty air conditioning. Then she decides it's pneumonia.
She grows weaker. She sees the doctor, who tells her to
quit smoking or don't come back because he won't be
responsible for her death. Then, through a course of events
no one can remember later on, she collapses from severe
acute hypertension and enters the hospital with her blood
pressure topping 200. Her kidneys fail. Her heart fails. Her
lungs fill with fluid; she almost drowns in bed. As doctors
pump out the hollows of her chest, Jeanne sits bolt upright
and says: "I haven't been good to God!!" She doesn't know

why she says this: "I haven't been good to God!!" She doesn't think she believes in God. She doesn't think she's been anything but agnostic for forty-some years.

Later, she thinks: Maybe I do believe in God. Maybe I've believed in God all along. Maybe being an agnostic means knowing that God's out there, however distant, gathering like a storm in coal-black bunches of cloud. The bolt strikes suddenly, but not without warning, not without cause. She thinks: I knew it was coming. I knew it would hit me. And I knew, when it struck, I would never be the same. Then she thinks: I wish I could have a cigarette. Damn.

*****

Mama was sick a lot. Colds, flus, stomach bugs, infections -- that's kids' stuff. When she got sick, she got SICK -- I mean in a life-threatening, high-opera, Puccini-Mimi-grab-the-hanky kind of way. Pneumonia? Check. Graves Disease? Check. (Her eyes popped out, then sank back; one sank back too far.) Gallstones? Check. Heart failure? Kidney failure? High blood pressure? Check Check Check. Skin cancer? Check. Strokes? Check. Gangrenous intestines? Check. She was so accustomed to almost dying (it's in the medical dictionary, under "A": Almostitis Dyingitria) that she tended to be on the blasé side when something awful happened to her. After her first stroke she called Lucy "Bob" (Lucy replied, "What do you want, Frank?"), then insisted on making supper despite an inability to talk; in the throes of her second she tried to order a hamburg with onions at a roadside joint but could only utter "ONION," yielding a plate of onion rings, which she loathed. She knew then she'd had a stroke, knew she ought to visit the hospital, but decided to pick up a few prescriptions at the New Preston Pharmacy first. There the pharmacist convinced her to phone an ambulance rather than drive herself ("My driving wasn't impaired, only my speech," she later explained). It's a miracle she lived as long as she did: She tended to pooh-pooh everything. When gangrene seized her insides she vomited blood, a fact she mentioned with no particular urgency in a late-night call to her doctor. He ordered her to the E. R.; she refused, saying she couldn't leave Louis alone in the house. This decent man drove out to the lake with his wife, picked up Mama and Daddy, took Mama to the hospital for immediate surgery and got Daddy admitted to a nursing home -- all in the middle of the night. By the time Lucy and I heard about it, Mama was in recovery. "So, she's dodged another bullet," said one of her lifelong friends, laughing. "She's dodged them all her life."

*****

After Mama died, Tamar helped me pick out a vase to bury her in. We found what we needed, a bold-stroke floral design with a heavy pine stopper, at a Pier 1 Imports outside Albany. With Lucy and Daddy we were stupid enough to pay hundreds of dollars for faux-marble petroleum-based "urns"; by the time Mama died we'd figured out that all anyone who's been reduced to ashes really needs is a jar. (Tamar and I deserve commendation for *not* buying a gaudy ceramic cat in which to inter my mother. We did come close.)

Equipped with this brilliant funereal crock, the four of us -- Chris and I, Tamar and baby Madeleine -- drove down to Mama's house the night before the burial and prepared to transfer her ashes from tin can to earthen vessel. A dramatic scene unfolded, reproduced with brutal honesty below.

AMY (holding tin): Guess we oughta open this thing.
TAMAR: Oh, here we go, Jeanne.
AMY (attempting to open tin): Oof.
TAMAR: Hmm.
CHRIS: Maybe if you hold your elbow up a little higher. .?
AMY: Oof.

TAMAR: Hmm.

MADELEINE (offstage): Waaaah!

AMY (to Chris): Oof, Honey, you do it.

CHRIS (opening tin): There.

AMY: Yay!

TAMAR: Yay!

CHRIS: And the vase. . . is. . .

AMY: Umm, over there, on the thingamajigee, right on
        the counter next to the jar of kumquats -- see?

CHRIS (picking up tin as though to pour; has a second
        thought): Amy, do you want to do this? It's
        your mother.

AMY: Okey-doke. (She starts to pour. Immediately
        a cloud of black cinder billows forth from the tin,
        engulfing everyone in a nebula of human remains
        and settling on the floor and kitchen surfaces like
        fine volcanic ash.)

TAMAR: Cough, cough.

AMY: Cough, hack, cough.

CHRIS: Hack, hack.

MADELEINE (offstage): Waaaaah!

AMY: Oh, my God, she's everywhere.

TAMAR: Ha ha!

CHRIS: Ha ha ha! Cough.

AMY: Cough, cough. Ha ha!

CHRIS: I'll get the vacuum. Cough.

TAMAR: I think there's some in the cat dish.

VACUUM
CLEANER:Ooorreeeeeeeeeeeeerrrrrroooeeeeeeeeer.

AMY: Ha ha! Sorry, Ma. Ha ha ha!

-- CURTAIN --

Mama had a few strange theories. She believed
noses and earlobes kept growing through adulthood until
death, and possibly after (although, for obvious reasons,
not in her case). She believed if you turned a photograph
upside down, you could divine the evil in someone's eyes -

- try it with the Ayatollah Khomeini. She believed Thomas Merton might have been a reincarnation of Johann Sebastian Bach, even though she didn't otherwise believe in reincarnation. She believed the trees talked at night; she figured this out as a child and swore up and down that scientists confirmed as much in the '70s. She was always quoting a vague consortium of scientists whose results she'd seen in a magazine, or heard on the radio, or watched on the evening news. Decades before the arrival of the information age she was Media Girl, a fast reader and unabashed tube-watcher who absorbed peculiar factoids for quick retrieval later on. Her command of minutiae was astounding -- she could describe the mating habits of obscure African grasshoppers AND deconstruct male actors and TV journalists whose careers waned "because their faces looked like bottoms." Back when carbo-loading was the rage among marathon runners, Mama took on a starch-intensive regimen to prepare for a recital; she told my friend Pam, who was pre-med at the time, that she had "eaten macaroni and cheese for two weeks -- do you think that's enough?"

Some folks might have called her gullible, but she wasn't. She didn't believe everything she heard. But what she believed, she believed with gusto -- God being the main beneficiary. She was a mystic as well as a pragmatist, a woman whose contemplative bent found expression in music long before she (and it) turned toward religion. No artist, no matter how skeptical or atheistic or nihilistic or unsure, can live free of mysticism, just as no house builder can make do without wood and nails. It's the stuff of the job, the stuff of interpretation and creation and fecund unfettered thought. From the moment she first lifted the fiddle to her chin she flirted with the supernatural – with the force, be it personal or impersonal, God or genius, that drives us to create. For years she assumed it was genius. But when she lay in bed at night, she believed the trees were talking.

*****

Mama's conversion gave us permission to talk about God. By "conversion" I mean not her entrance into Catholicism at the age of 60 but the period eight or nine years earlier, in the aftermath of that agnostic's epiphany. She knew she had found God in I.C.U. but wasn't sure whose. So she looked about her. She looked at the Tibetan Book of the Dead, at the Koran, the Bible, the writings of Elisabeth Kübler-Ross. She looked at Moody's *Life After Life*, at spiritualism, at Celtic mythology and the mystery of Stonehenge. She read C.S. Lewis. She read Merton. She read accounts of out-of-body experiences -- *Return From Tomorrow*, by George S. Ritchie, was a favorite. All of these things she discussed with us, and down many of these paths Lucy and I (not Daddy – never Daddy) hesitantly followed. Slowly, incrementally, not in some violent flash of comprehension but in a band of light much softer and less discrete, we began to believe in a glorious elsewhere. We began to believe that life embraced more than the breadths of our arms. Our shoe sizes, our braincases, our senses, our strides: More than that.

I don't know when this understanding struck my mother, and I don't know when it struck me; I only know that by the time I turned 16, Mama and Lucy and I believed in something. By the time I graduated, we were all churchgoing Christians. People often speak of the "slippery slope" in a negative moral sense, as a dislodged pebble that kicks off a landslide and propels us rump-first into the licking fires of Gehenna. But God can send us tumbling down His own slope just as easily, just as furtively. All it takes is that first something – that first squishy inkling of an Other, whether here or there, omnipotent or scattered. Something. Atheists be warned: It doesn't take much, only a moment's gasp at the sight of an infant's fingers, only a Why asked once as the sun spills rose into the dusk. For me it might have been the Ode to Joy – that crazy syncopation in the winds. Just a pebble.

Mama scuffled first down the slope, then Lucy, then me in the rear (the procrastinator). Mama's conversion seemed extraordinary to us all, became more extraordinary as the years passed and she told us more about it. At the start she was simply curious and read to feed her curiosity; she wanted to know what sort of God had roused her. Later on she was assailed by regret: not regret in the broad self-help sense, but a very specific regret that had nothing to do with her inner Shamecore. She regretted the errors she'd made in her adult life and wanted only to apologize to the boss. I don't know whether the word "sin" had penetrated her vocabulary by then, but I do know that she entered an empty church one afternoon, sat down in a pew and asked aloud, "How can I be forgiven?" Immediately she heard a reply in a voice not her own: "You already are."

Mama confessed to this a decade later, well after I'd turned into a bit of a Jesus freak myself. I believed her unhesitatingly; I still do. This is the sort of divine moment that can't be minimized or denied, but it's still tough to own up to such things. God Hath Spoken. Isn't that what she'd said? In a different typeface? Minus the "Hath"? The Almighty has never chatted with me directly, and if He did, I'm not sure I'd tell people; I'd be afraid of the funny looks I'd get in reply. But enough peculiar things have happened in my orbit (note chapters 1, 2, 3, 4 and 6) that I tend to give the benefit of the doubt to anyone who claims an encounter with the supernatural.

Lucy said she saw God, and nothing I know about either party – her or Him (or Her?) – made me think she was lying. Either her epilepsy made her believe she saw God, or she saw God; or else the sight of God caused her epilepsy. Maybe that's how brains behave under the circumstances. In the same way, either Mama's anguish made her believe she heard God, or she heard God. Regardless of the cause, the result was revelation and profound spiritual change.

Mama had one more epiphany, some years after

the first. It struck while she was driving a woodsy back-route home to Connecticut late one night after a day trip to buy sheet music in Manhattan. Two things happened. 1) She started to sob. 2) She got lost. Mama knew that route as well as any, but this time she lost her way amid the whorly roads and midnight clutch of branches. Curling county lane led to curling county lane led to a complete loss of bearings, figurative and literal. She didn't know why she was crying. She didn't know how she got lost. She didn't know where she was, or how to get home, or what to make of her own distress. Shaking with tears, she pulled into the first evidence of civilization she found: a sign for the Abbey of Regina Laudis, a Benedictine convent in southern Litchfield County. She parked her car, pondered the rustic cloister, entered a small anteroom, rang the bell and waited. Up to a wooden grate popped a nun in full habit. Deo Gratias, the nun said. Mama said, I've been driving. I've been driving and I'm lost and I made mistakes in my life and I made a lot of them and I can't stop crying and I need to talk to someone and can I talk to you and what town is this, anyway? The nun said, Bethlehem. Mama said, Bethlehem, oh. The nun said, I'm not a priest, I can't give absolution. Mama said, I'm not Catholic anyway. The nun said, But you can talk and I can listen. And maybe you'll find the way.

Mama talked, and the nun listened. So began friendships -- with the intuitive Mother Placid, with the gracious, insightful Mother Ruth -- that lasted until Mama's death. So, too, began her passage toward Catholicism, a rambling turn that paralleled Lucy's and inspired (after a protracted stretch of foot-shuffling) mine.

*****

She was wise: She was Solomon, minus the baby. When I wanted to hear the truth about something, I went to Mama. When I didn't, I shut my mouth and kept it shut and made sure she didn't pry it open. Unsentimental to the end, she loved hard and forever, but she didn't hang on to the meaningless threads and scraps that people leave behind. She saw friends and relatives for what they were and loved them anyway. She was brutal and accepting, of others and herself. "May you never have a worse problem," she'd say when I was whiny. "Your eyes are two burnt holes in a blanket,'' she'd say when I was tired. Or: "Don't let money burn a hole in your pocket." Or: "You need him (her/them/it/that/those) like you need a hole in the head.''

A hole in the head. She died of a hole in the head. Is that funny, er what?

Her favorite sayings involved holes in the head, or the brain, or the mind, or the dirt. Digging, always digging – into her own thinking, into ours, into the garden to plant impatiens. "Well, well, well, three holes in the ground,'' she liked to say to say. And: "That's better than a hole in the head!'' And: "There's such a thing as being so open minded that your brains fall out.'' This last quip she reserved for extreme moral liberalism, which she regarded as essentially moronic – for the same reason she regarded extreme social conservatism as essentially cruel. It was too much. Love one another, love the poor, engage in whatever causes will lead to a better world -- but keep your skirt down and your pants up, would you? And don't take drugs. They'll put a hole in your head, for sure.

She said other things. When faced with a violent difference of opinion, she said, "That's why there's chocolate and vanilla,'' then addressed her bag of jelly beans, which were neither. When faced with multiple problem-solving stratagems, she said, "There's more than one way to skin a cat,'' a fairly shocking statement from such an avowed fan of the species. When faced with a daughter in a droopy mood, she said, "You have a half-warmed fish inside of you," reflecting her lifelong fondness for spoonerisms ("You have a half-formed wish inside of you"). When the half-warmed fish involved a boy, she said, "Whatever you do, don't fall in love with a lamppost,'' which of course we usually did. (You need him like you need a hole in the etc., etc.) And when infatuation left one of us broken-hearted and spindled by shame, she said, simply, "Guilt sucks." She swore she was going to get T-shirts made with that logo: "Guilt sucks." She believed it, wanted us to believe it, too. Guilt sucks.

When Lucy died, Mama felt guilty. Felt guilty because the two of them had been arguing in the last weeks of Lucy's life. Felt guilty because their final conversation had ended with an abrupt and angry exchange. Felt guilty because Mama was taking a bath the Saturday evening before Lucy killed herself and she heard the telephone ring and ring and ring, figuring it was Lucy, debating whether to answer it, deciding finally not to. Felt guilty because she loved Lucy and worked hard to keep her alive and felt it was her job, just as it was her job to take care of Louis and keep him out of a nursing home – another failure, in her book. So many failures. So many causes for guilt. Guilt sucks. Guilt utterly, unreservedly, irrefutably, existentially, cosmically sucks. I believe she came to terms with it by the end of her life, but only in the sense that someone comes to terms with a bum knee. It didn't go away; she learned to accept it. On some level Mama knew that she had tried her best – God knows how many eleventh-hour runs she made to Boston, determined to comfort and save her suffering eldest daughter – and knew that in the end, it was up to Lucy to keep herself alive. Up to God to stay her hand or help her. The curse of suicide isn't simply the loss of a loved one, or the bluffness of it, or the ghastly self-hatred that leads to it. The true, lingering horror is the onus it places on those who survive – the blame that weighs on everyone who might have intervened but didn't, couldn't, wouldn't. I live and Lucy does not. Which inaction of mine led to her death? Which action? Which words, said or unsaid?

Ah, to hell with it. Or, no: to heaven with it. After Lucy died I was struck at once by the newness of life around me -- maybe it was spring, maybe it was the hope (mine, Mama's, Lucy's) that my embattled sister had been

reborn in light. I felt it again after Daddy died, and again
with Mama. It's an unexpected paradox -- this conviction,
amid all the mourning, that somehow life can triumph, that
somehow the busywork of our little human needs and our
little human ways can bring us stumbling to glory. Friends
sometimes ask how I dealt with the pain of three major
losses in two short years, and I'm never quite sure how to
answer. Life only moves in one direction: That's the beauty
of it. It zigs and zags; it rises and dips; it careers like a
drunk; it slows to a crawl. But it only goes forward, just as
Mama only went forward, driving along bendy roads in her
bouncing foreign car, steering around potholes and ice
slicks and baby frogs and chipmunks, seeing only the
curve ahead through a double shaft of headlights in the
darkness. I learned from Mama that you can only drive to
the next bend -- on an unfamiliar road, that's all you've got,
so keep to the right and be ready to brake if necessary. It
was a good lesson: Don't look ahead too far. Don't try to
see around the curve. Just trundle along. Just stick it in
gear. Just go.

  I snapped a picture of my mother, just months
before her death, as she looked at her infant granddaughter
on a table before her. The photo was taken from the side,
so you can only see Mama's smile in profile -- but it's a
beautiful, wistful smile, slightly pursed, deeply knowing.
There's an edge of grief around it, a shadow cast by Lucy's
suicide a year and a half before. It's hard for me to look at.
But I love this photo, not only because it reminds me of
those seven placid months when my mother shared life
with my first child, but because I remember her words as
she smiled. "I thought there was no more joy for me in this
world," she said, and I knew she had found it at last.

6

Credo

I had thought this was a book about them. I had thought
this was a book about everyone but me -- uninteresting me,
me of the moderate character and sturdy gait. I had thought
I could write about my immoderate family, with their
surplus personalities and mystical bents, and leave myself
well out of it. I had thought I could remain a supporting
player, no more than a narrator or chorus. I had thought
that this wasn't even a memoir, believing it was biography
or portraiture rather than autobiography or self-portrait.
How baffled I was by those who read the book and said
they wanted more Me. More Me? Isn't this enough?
Personally, knowing Me as well as I do, I can confirm that
a small quantity of Me will go a long way; I'm none too
alluring a figure, with my abstemious nature and
dismayingly conservative life choices. For God's sake: I've

never even been drunk. Hoo-boy. Can't wait to read that memoir. Best-seller in the making.

Yet here I am, here Me is, forcing myself to stare a little harder at the contours of my past. I've looked at it, if only for a glimpse: My past is Their past, though I've worked hard at pretending it isn't. I've spent my sentient life trying to yank myself away from my family, to prove that I'm apart from it as much as I'm a part of it. I need to believe that I'm different, that I can define myself in separate terms. I tried to remove myself from this book as I tried to remove myself from my family. I fancied myself an outsider. I fancied that I could whisk Amy away into a bland, Biancolli-free zone where everyone wears sober ties and talks about mortgage rates; or perhaps I fancied that I could whisk them away, as though they hadn't left already.

As a child I always measured myself against my parents and sister. I was never as smart, never as gifted, never as sick. By no reckoning did my strengths and weaknesses stack up against theirs, though they made themselves hoarse telling me how talented I was, what a Good Mind, what a fine Monopoly player! And look at Amy on that pogo stick -- terrific! I didn't believe them, but bless them anyway. I, the youngest, simplest Biancolli to set foot on the cluttered shores of Waramaug -- what hope did I have? I dwelt on my singular lack of singularity and understood it, finally, as a kind of salvation. I defined myself not by who I was but who I wasn't, as though ordinariness could be built up between us like the walls of a protective dike. The flood was over there. I was over here. I stood very very far away. See how my clothes stayed dry?

One night at the supper table -- I was in high school, I think -- my mother said a neighbor had spotted me on the front lawn, juggling a soccer ball. "Amy plays soccer?" he asked, as though the notion of Biancollis running around in satin shorts was too much to bear. "Yes, she's very good," responded Mama, who always liked to shock friends with tales of her vagabond younger daughter.

Recounting this conversation, she turned to me across the Spinach Oregano and added: "You're the normal one, kiddo. You save our reputation."

Normal: I liked that word. I liked to hear it applied to me. I liked anything or anyone that implicitly or explicitly pointed to a total absence of irregularity. On a raw physical level, I'd always enjoyed sports -- soccer most of all, but baseball and basketball as well -- and I liked what they implied. Normal kids played ball; abnormal kids practiced the piano four and a half hours a day. I played outfield and even caught a fly ball, once. My teammates cheered. My coach smiled at me. Normal. Cool.

"And what do YOU play?" asked someone, anyone, inevitably after a recital by Mama or Lucy, turning a foreshortened nose in my direction. Likely as not I played nothing, having abandoned the violin at 13 and the piano at 6. But before I could work up a flush of embarrassment, Mama rescued me: "Amy plays sports. Amy plays soccer," she'd say, smiling. "Plus, she's quite a poet!" And then the blush would rise, and I would roll my eyes, and I would hang my bangs-plagued head, and in my best pubescent pique, I'd moan, *Maaaaaaaaaaaa.*

For Lucy's senior piano recital at Wykeham Rise I wore a frilly white polyester dress with puffy sleeves and baby-blue trim. It was hideous. It made me itch. Desperate, with barely twenty minutes to go before the concert, I asked my friend Tonya if she wanted to go play catch in the parking lot. There we were, tossing a softball back and forth, my petroleum-based party dress huffing in the wind, when Wykeham's front door opened to emit my curious mother. I'll never forget her face when she saw me: worried, surprised, annoyed, incongruously proud. She knew I had tried to escape.

I was always making a getaway of some sort. More than once, I jumped from a moving car in the midst of a row with Mama. As a kid I ran away from home several times, never making it farther than the weeping willows at the bottom of the hill before regret over Mama and

Daddy's worry pulled me gently back.

Even then I felt the need to escape, felt the need to be an outsider in my own family. It's a scary thing, being a Biancolli; the ramifications are terrifying. Every once in a while, when I give my emotions a little too much play on the leash, I begin to think I'm doomed. You remember doom: It rhymes with loom and gloom, and it irks me. The problem with it, and me, is that I start feeling as though a melodramatic psychiatric breakdown is genealogically pre-ordained; I start feeling as though I have a razor-horned mini-Biancolli sitting on my left shoulder, whispering demonic nothings in my ear and warning me, in his raspy countertenor, that I'm destined for a life of long-term hospitalizations and untold psychotropic drugs. Such visions are nothing more than morbid fantasy, but it's hard to grow up and away from a family like mine without regarding mental illness as a normal state of affairs. Because of this, I tend to fear my own strong feelings, strongly expressed, as a harbinger of Zoloft to come; I tend to misinterpret normal affective tides as evidence of a flood.

"Am I like Lucy?" I ask my husband. "Am I like Daddy? Am I mentally ill? Am I depressed?" He always says no, and I always believe him -- he's an honest man with an orderly mind and an un-Mediterranean lack of sentimentality, and if he thought his wife were cracking up, he'd say so. He also loves me, and while he recognizes and celebrates the bright ribbon of Biancolliana in my soul, he loves me in part because I've broken away from my parents and sister; he loves that I have sworn off mayhem, or at least tried to.

And the older I get, the more inspiration I find in the memory of my sane mother, who was the one true ballast amid the storming dysfunction of my childhood. Though she had a temper, particularly in the days before her hypertension was diagnosed and treated, she wasn't depressed or unbalanced; she was merely a good woman with big emotions in a marriage to a powerfully strange man. The lunacy around her tried and bent her, but she never broke. She rolled up her sleeves and fought off the blows as best she could, defending her own well-being along with her children's. In the months and years after my father attempted suicide, she reassured me and Lucy that it wasn't our fault -- "It's nothing you did. He's the one who did it," she'd say, whenever she thought we'd listen. I'm not sure Lucy heard her, but I did, and this sharp rebuke of my father's behavior was a lesson I never forgot.

His hospitalization was a difficult time for me, a stretch of six months when I plucked out my eyelashes one by one and developed noisy bedtime tics that kept my sister awake. I was, at age 11, a sad kid; my school portrait from 6th grade, which Daddy kept in the top drawer of his dresser, showed a pale, exhausted child with bald eyelids and a face that looked weak from the effort of smiling. And yet I listened when Mama told me I was a good girl and had done nothing to make my father sick; I listened when Daddy said he loved me, and I never thought he didn't. I seemed to understand, even then, even as a hurting child, that my father's insanity was his own inscrutable business, that even he couldn't figure it out, and that his love for his family was, in some way, unimpeachable and exempt. It was his one great Fact, a reality that couldn't be doubted. My mother saw this: It's why she didn't take her girls and leave. She saw that we could live together and be whole as a family if Daddy's sickness were sifted from his love and set aside, a poisonous byproduct separate from the irreducible whole. He Is Crazy But He Loves You, she said. Never Think He Doesn't Love You. He's Only Crazy. You Are Not.

I am not.

I do not want to die. I do not want to cut my arms until they bleed and scar. I do not want to leave this life for a better one, for I find this one fine enough. I do not want to sleep all day. I do not want to intoxicate myself with sorrow or Seconal or death. I do not see things that aren't there, or hear things that haven't spoken, or act in a

trembling fugue on memories that never were. I do not
threaten to kill myself in front of my kids. I open my eyes
and see a foursquare life: sometimes easy, sometimes hard.
I love my husband and do not want to hurt him. I love my
children and do not want to leave them; I want them to
grow complacent with my love, to know that I am here,
always, loving them predictably, loving them well. I do not
want to hate myself -- for their sake, or for mine. I want to
be stable. I want to be sane. I want my life with my young
family to be as predictable and safe as my life with my old
one was unpredictable and fraught with risk.

Like Mama, I'm a pragmatist. I understand that
contentment is nine-tenths behavior, and somewhere along
the line I decided to be okay -- I started acting like a happy
person, and so I became one. How simplistic this sounds: I
smiled, and, wow, I felt great! Clearly I was not clinically
depressed, or this would not have worked. But it did work,
and it does work, and on days when a gray shroud nears, I
force myself to step outside and chat with my neighbors --
thank God I live in a city, pressed up against other human
beings, or my head would fall off with self-absorption.

Which makes me wonder: Would the Biancollis
have been the Biancollis if they'd lived on a densely
populated dead-end street in a small urban center? Would
they have screamed as much, or cried as much, or wrapped
themselves as thickly in their sadness? Would Daddy have
retreated to his bedroom, would Lucy have retreated to her
mind? I don't know: We had neighbors on the Lake, good
ones, present ones, and there is surely no dearth of
madmen in metropolises. But if I am the "normal
Biancolli," if I am successful and content in this normalcy,
I have city living to thank for it, at least in part: It pushes
me into the shared space of sidewalks and public schools
and kids thwacking street pucks with cubbish enterprise.
Inside my home I can mope all I want, but out on the
pavement I have to smile at the mailman, the moms, the
stay-at-home dad with the cover band and the hi-top
Converse All-Stars. Hey, George, howzitgoin, I say,

nudging the stroller toward the corner, and George says: Look at Mitchell, see how big he's getting.

And George and I talk about U2, or B.F. Skinner, or stomach bugs. And Alicia comes out with her youngest, and Andrea across the street has her toddler in a backpack and her preschooler in a watermelon dress. And we gab, and we smile, and the kids run around, and when the 6'1" teenager with the fresh Irish face lopes up, we say, Hey Brian, and Brian says Hey and lopes on past, and Brian's mother comes out on her porch and we say, Rose, that kid of yours, he's so tall, and Rose says: You should see him eat. And we all smile and laugh until finally I say, Gotta pick up the girls from school, and I nudge the stroller down the street, and down another street, and down five more streets, and then I'm outside the girls' school waiting for them to emerge and I'm smiling and chatting with the Muslim dad and the husk-blond dad and the Chinese mom and the Indian mom and the Croatian dad and the Russian granddad and the working mom and the single mom and the amazing ultra-volunteer mom and one or two lesbian moms and the genially cranky head janitor, whose crankiness is just a put-on but earns him a vulgar graffito scraped into a square of concrete in front of the twin front doors. And the doors open, and the girls run out, and hundreds of other kids run out, and they're all smiling and laughing and running and attacking each other and nearly killing each other, but smiling and laughing all the same. And I smile and I laugh. And I'm fine.

This is my life: Perfecting the actions of normalcy. I am at heart a person of balance, but I am determined to maintain that balance through an exacting regimen of drop biscuits, Girl Scout meetings and laundry. I love being a mom; I'm sure I would love being a mom if I were suicidal or intensely delusional or both, but I love it even more knowing that I'm not. Knowing that this lovely, quotidian existence of mine is so far removed from the very un-quotidian layout of my youth. Knowing that it frees me from living in the past, for my children demand that I live for the future. Knowing that I am acting out a long-cherished dream, a dream of being not one of Those Biancollis but just Amy, just a writer and mother on her own small terms, just me. A few people in Albany met Mama before she died, but no one here met Lucy or Daddy. To them I am no one but my present self. I am complete without parents and sister. I am one, and that is enough.

*****

       Loss has a settling effect on one's mind: It sorts out priorities with a quiet, humming logic. In the years since my family's deaths, their absence has clarified every moment of crisis, every stab of love. Grief fades over time -- it takes on the properties of distance, reducing in vividness and size -- but it never disappears, and it never ceases to be relevant. In my case, it's a reality check, an insistent jab in the ribs whenever I'm tempted by self-pity; it reminds me to be grateful, to treasure what I have and stay cognizant, always, of life's outrageous impermanence. My little son nurses, his fingers stretching and clenching at my breast, and I frame the moment in my mind before it passes. My younger daughter asks me to stroke her brow at bedtime, and I crawl in next to her, laying my cool palm across her forehead with the remembered love of my mother laying hers across mine. I feel my older daughter's hand grasp mine on the walk to school, a last spasm of babyhood before the suspicious grip of puberty takes hold. Days split into hours split into seconds split into half-seconds and ever-smaller increments of time, yet the smallest of these leap into timelessness with the hazy import of revelation. I know I am not here permanently, just as my father and sister and mother were not here permanently; I know I will bury my husband, or he will bury me. It is a dreadful knowledge. But there is beauty to be found in it, awe to be felt in it, if I embrace its transience as a splinter of infinity, a short gulp of breath in the unending intake of creation. I don't know how I would cope with this life if I didn't believe in another one; I would again be like a child, and fear the shapeless dark.

*****

Near the end of the beautiful, evocative *Hunger of Memory: The Education of Richard Rodriguez*, the author ponders his half-naked reflection, marveling at the transformation from insecure child to muscular, capable adult. I have no such moment of unflinching self-regard to offer. I also have no desire to stare at myself unclothed in the mirror, having given birth three times and witnessed the blob-like after-effects on my figure. But if I did, which I won't, so you'll have to take my word for it, not that you wouldn't, I would note the following characteristics, rated "G" for general audiences:

Height: 5'4", although recent doctor's visit unexpectedly shrank me .5 inches; weight: somewhere around 145 pounds, much of it distributed in large muscle groups in thighs, overdeveloped from eight years of competitive soccer; similar overdevelopment in calves and ankles, lyrically celebrated by man on mountain bike in Manhattan's fashion district, autumn 1986, with "You have big legs! I like big legs! You have big legs!"; scarring on midsection from pregnancy; bulging features to east and west of midsection, distantly distinguishable as "hips"; protuberant, knob-shaped knees, scarred internally by soccer, externally by sociopathic second-grader who pushed me repeatedly on the playground; square hands -- inherited from mother; double-jointed thumbs, which can reach behind knuckle of index finger -- inherited from father; long neck; long arms; round head; big jaw, remarked upon by orthodontist/torturer of four years -- inherited from mother; big teeth, mostly straight, thanks to orthodontist/torturer of four years; long, straight nose; small ears; dark eyes deep-set under thick smudges of eyebrow, a combo that prompted Tea Leoni, attending a press junket, to tell me that I "look like Maximilian Schell" -- inherited from father; light olive complexion -- inherited from father; thick hair fast on its way from near-black to gray, a spectral shift first noted at age 16; a face devoid of make-up and sleep, serious in repose but easily brightened; and the overall impression of wiped-out contentedness, of a mother in her early middle age, occupied, distracted, tired but peaceful, maybe a bit wilted around the edges, but happy to make the meatloaf nonetheless.

I am so relieved to be getting older. It's a gift: It means I'm one step closer to living out my life without catastrophe. I complain about my aches and blemishes, but I feel thrilled and privileged to complain about them. Every sag and wrinkle is a sag or wrinkle Lucy didn't earn. Every stretch mark is a reminder of my blessings. If my body is scarred by joy, if it feels the weight of its accumulated living, then I must hang up my pride and pray for many more decades of deterioration and age. I hope to God I live long enough to turn into an old bag, to see my children mature and marry and have kids and maybe grandkids and whine to their shrinks about my failings. I want to give them what I didn't have -- parents who overstay their welcome, a family that doesn't die. I want to give them normal.

And I have, I think, so far. But my urge to give my children all that I didn't have is tempered by a parallel urge to give them all that I did have -- all the music, all the words, all the runneth-over affection and infectious bouts of laughter. I am proud to hail from a long line of eccentrics. That's one reason I've been unable to purge me from my family or my family from me: I could never truly let them go, not in my mind or on these pages. Not even as a literary exercise -- or literary exorcism -- could I cast off the ghosts of the Biancollis. They're in me, and I in them, forever.

*****

I'm not dead. I've never been dead, though I've come close once or twice -- maybe three times, but who's counting? Except me, and rest assured, I am counting. The first was that time Lucy and I were clawing the sheer drop off Arthur's Seat and I panicked in a large way and refused to let go of my adorable sheep-covered brollie and Lucy had to calm me down before I hyperventilated myself into a coma (a coma! ack!) and tumbled off the cliff into oblivion. Then there was the time the impact from a head-on collision (someone else's) sent a crumpled ball of steel, formerly a car, hurtling in my direction, only to land twenty feet in front of me and shower my windshield with glass. Then again there was the time I had a supraventricular tachycardia in the middle of a Tanglewood performance, probably a reaction to some errant Debussy, and my heart wouldn't slow down from 200-odd beats per minute and after an hour my face went numb and on a subsequent ambulance ride to Berkshire Medical Center a paramedic gave me a drug that stopped my heart. Stopped my heart. During which I felt a cold black hand seize my body for a second or two of intense all-encompassing pain before my heart fired up again thank God.

But that's about it. No irreversible brushes with the big one. Not yet.

As a result, I have no first-hand knowledge of the afterlife. I've never seen God. I've never heard God, spoken with God, spotted God in a milling crowd or recognized the back of His head in a movie theater. I've never encountered angels or shmoozed with dead folk who materialized at the foot of my bed. I've never "seen the light,'' "embraced the light,'' been "saved by the light,'' or otherwise been sucked down an illuminated tunnel into the waiting arms of eternity. I've never even repented, not in the conventional sense, although I suppose I must have when my childish atheism gave way to a sapling faith. Whenever that was. Like I could remember it happening.

I remember my mother's, father's and sister's conversions well enough -- Mama's was dramatic, Daddy's miraculous, Lucy's saintly -- but my own lacked character, just as I lacked character, just as everything I did or said or dreamed lacked the vivid bizarrerie of my unusual family. Their gifts were extravagant, their conversions wide awake. With my modest stirrings I felt tiny by comparison, but I was too busy standing on their shoulders to resent them for being giants. They gave me too much, taught me too much, brought me to too many places -- I was along for the ride. That's probably why I can't recall my own startled moment of belief: It was simply an outgrowth of theirs. Just as Lucy gave me her love of Brahms and Mama gave me her arsenal of handy two-letter Scrabble words (ai, en, em, fa), they each gave me the language -- the idioms -- of faith. With them I heard faith speak and saw how it behaved. I learned about the Bible. I learned about mysticism, monotheism, temptation, God and devil, heaven and hell. I learned about the divine Jesus, as opposed to the good-guy Jesus we'd all known in years past. When Lucy and Mama started praying, so did I -- wordlessly, embarrassedly, at night in the dark with the bed sheets over my head. How old I was, I don't recall. I don't recall the final moment of disbelief or the first clear moment of belief. I don't recall the day I stopped fearing death. I don't recall the shuddering micro-second when I realized I was no longer a skeptic, when I felt the red well up in my cheeks from a slap by the hand of God.

But look at me: a blubbering fool for the Lord. Non-believers take aim, for here writes the Avenging Proselytizing Atomizing Energizing Discombobulated Neurotic Convert FROM HELL! -- but "hell" is too strong a word. FROM PURGATORY! After Lucy and Mama converted to Catholicism I spent a long time adamantly not doing the same, mainly because I didn't want to imitate them. I even tried anti-Catholicism on for size, as though getting snitty about papist doctrine would somehow protect me from its influences. You might say I was confused. This period coincided with my devout-generic-Christian phase in college, when I was attending Protestant services on weekends and becoming obsessed with the super-Catholic fiction of Graham Greene and Flannery O'Connor during the week. I especially liked O'Connor's story "Greenleaf," in which a bull wearing a crown of thorns gores a cynical farm owner. A nice metaphor for conversion, yes?

After college I spent a year in Scotland and became equally obsessed with Jewish history, tradition and authors, from Chaim Potok to Martin Buber. Let me explain: I was living in a Protestant nation. All year long I attended Church of Scotland services, and all year long I heard very little Old Testament scripture. Most likely this was peculiar to the two churches I attended in Edinburgh, and the last thing I want to do is generalize condescendingly about the teachings or liturgy of any Protestant sect. But the fact is I found myself craving the Hebrew Bible and the faith of the Israelites. I realized I needed the Jews. I needed my faith – my Christianity, my understanding of Jesus – to be rooted in the wisdom and sacrifices of God's chosen people.

This is the closest I ever came to revelation, this inching toward the ancient stock of worship, and had I not believed in the divinity of Christ I might have converted to Judaism in my early twenties. But it was as a Christian that I loped down a steep Edinburgh hill one unusually clear spring day, and as the sun streaked across Princes Street Gardens I understood that I would someday be Catholic. For Catholicism emphasized the Eucharist above all: the awesome, awful miracle of Jesus' sacrifice, reenacted billions upon billions of times in the two millennia since the final Passover of his life. Jesus the Paschal lamb, the Passover lamb, the swipe of his blood filling chalices at the Christian altar. Catholics don't shrink from the mess of it all – from the earthy, sticky, gaudy-bleeding-plaster-statue fact of it. You can't be squeamish when you sit in those pews; you can't deny the dirt under your fingernails; and you can't ignore the Christian's debt to Judaism, which gave us the language of triumph and loss. And who first loved the God who made us.

That's it. That's why I'm Catholic. I spent years afterward in a funk of noodly procrastination, years of attending Mass without receiving communion or making myself known to any priest. I was afraid that committing to one religion meant having to dismiss all others as false. This anxiety worsened one Good Friday in the late 1980s, when I accompanied Mama to Mass at her parish church and left in tears after the pastor regaled his lambs with an idiotic screed on "the one true Church." I just wanted to worship Christ on the cross on a day when sectarianism shouldn't reign. He was telling me I couldn't. Mama, led by wisdom or angels, drove around Northwestern Connecticut looking for another Good Friday service and found a small wooden church in Bethlehem, just a mile or two from her nuns. As we entered the Mass ended and congregants poured out. Inside the priest was hearing confessions. Mama waited her turn, then pulled the curtain behind her. I sat in the pews and prayed, for what I don't remember.

A few minutes later, Mama came out. She gave me a kiss and slid into a pew across the aisle. The pastor, a convert from England, sat beside me.

I waited. He waited. Finally, he said: "Did you want to ask me about something?" -- his vows having barred him from revealing the content of his talk with Mama. He had to hear it from me first.

I told him about the other priest, at the other church, and the shame and anger I felt at his remarks. Did I have to be Catholic to love Christ? I asked. Was my faith in God invalid just because I hadn't yet converted?

This is what he said. He said: We all worship the same God, the same Christ, and only this one God knows when and how you will convert to Catholicism.

He said: I converted as a young man. My mother

did not convert until the end of her life. If you feel led to the Church, you will become Catholic in God's time and yours.

He said again: We all worship the same Christ.

And then he left, and I wept again. Mama told me later that the priest, whose name I can't remember and whose church I never revisited, had a look on his face when he left me that said he'd been touched by God. "He looked stunned, like he didn't know where his words had come from," she said. "He was outside of himself."

Another year passed, and then another. In the Boston area I attended Tip O'Neill's old parish, then switched to a massive church at the bottom of my street for no other reason than I could walk to it. It was half a block away; I had no excuse not to. After work each day I biked home from Harvard Square, charging down Massachusetts Avenue past the funeral home that handled Lucy's body two years later. Near the western boundary of North Cambridge I cut through a parking lot and up a narrow walkway past the church, turning up the street into Somerville and, fifty yards beyond, my home. On one such trip I barreled around the church path only to find myself face-to-face with the startled pastor. As it happens, I didn't knock him flat; instead, I half-fell off the bike, righted myself and said, breathless with exertion, "Oh! Father! I'd like to become a Catholic!"

Looking as though I *had* knocked him flat, Father Arthur Wright introduced himself and suggested I call the rectory for an appointment. And so I did, and so he told me, in the low light of an autumn afternoon, that there are many paths to God and that Catholicism is but one of them. Over the next few months I would take a course in adult instruction, he said, and at the end of the course I would, with God's will, receive my first Holy Communion as a Catholic at the Easter Vigil. But before that happened I must decide if this Catholic path to God is my path to God: He said that. And when he said that, I knew that it was.

My path has led me here, to this moment in this room -- an attic, drab with March -- in this fretful state of mind. The central characters of my childhood happen to be dead, which means that I am the central living witness to their stories.

So I write. I tell not all, but some: a Tell-Some Book. And I wonder at my own candor, my willingness to throw open the gates of public scrutiny on a topic that's so intensely personal. I'm writing about my family – their lives, deaths, illnesses and conversions. I'm writing about God. God! I'm telling the world that my mother heard the Almighty! And my sister saw Him! And I forgot to ask her what He looked like! And my father saw his late, dead daughter in his hospital room! And I had a prophetic dream before my mother died! And it starred William Shatner! And I expect the world to take me seriously from now on!

Blame my father -- isn't that what we're all supposed to do? Blame Dad? While he lay in that small Connecticut hospital, he in no uncertain terms instructed me to write about his deathbed conversion. Granted, he was semi-conscious and pre-occupied with visions of the next world, but still: The charge came clear as a bell. I walked into his room and he turned his head, looked me square in the eye. "Have you contacted anyone yet?'' he asked.

"Contacted anyone?''

"Yes -- have you contacted anyone yet?''

"About what, Daddy?''

"About writing about it.'' Anxiety flicked across his face -- he was worried that I hadn't gotten the point. And I hadn't.

"Writing about what?''

"About this,'' he said simply.

"This?''

"This,'' he said. His gaze traced the hospital room, his bed, down at himself. "All of this. All of what's happened.''

"Oh. No, not yet," I said.

Driving home later that evening, I pulled to the shoulder and rummaged around until I found a notebook. On its pages I recorded everything my father had said in the previous weeks – his encounter with Lucy, his remarks about God and Jesus and the bright light in the room with him, his "fantastic expansion of love.'' Once home I started writing. And when my father died ten days later, I finished the essay, printed it out and shipped it off to several newspapers, including the fine weekly in Connecticut where my good friend Toni Bosco gave me my start in journalism. Toni ran the piece, which led to a second piece that was published in an anthology two years later, which encouraged me to write about my sister in the Albany *Times Union*. Which led to this. Have you contacted anyone about writing about it, my father asked. Yes, I can now respond. Yes, you know, I have.

One late night not long ago I asked my husband if I was mad. I asked him if I was a selfish crackpot to write about my family. I asked him if I was exploiting their memory each time I told another story. "They went through so much, and here I am, telling the world,'' I said.

His reply stopped me cold.

"Maybe they went through so much,'' he said, "so you could tell the world.''

*****

Year after year, my parents and sister shouldered their burdens – burdens of responsibility, loss, disease. Always disease: Biancollis kept the pharmaceutical companies in business. Lucy alone was a walking primer on neuropsychopharmacology, a living, dying experiment in the (in)efficacy of antidepressants. You name it, she was on it, though probably not for long. She belonged to a drug-of-the-month club for chronic psych patients; you should see the tote bag she got when she joined.

Amid all this illness, I was the wobbly center. Of the four people in my immediate childhood family, I am the only one who has never been in a coma. So familiar to me is the sight of a loved one poked through with I.V.s and catheters and mysterious dribbling things that I treat with suspicion the good health of my friends and family now. It all seems so unreliable, this life, their health, my health; in the midst of my Debussy tachycardia I half-expected to land in intensive care with tubes up my nose. It's the Biancolli way.

Still, it's never been *my* way – not so far, anyway, although I'm just paranoid enough to suspect I'm dead-in-a-heap waiting to happen. My burden amid all that burdensome illness was to be the one not afflicted. As a child I visited Mama in intensive care, I visited Daddy in intensive care, I visited Daddy in the psych hospital afterward. As an adult I kept right on visiting. When Lucy attempted suicide for the first time, Mama stayed with her for a week in Cambridge while I drove Daddy home to Connecticut and fed him peas and fish sticks. His favorite meal: Every night I cooked it and every night he gobbled it up, forgetting that I'd served it to him just the day before. "Sayyyy. . . . Amigiiita. . . these are gooooood. What do you call them?'' "Peas and fish sticks, Daddy.'' "They're delicious! What a cook you are!'' A year later to the week Mama was back in intensive care -- those gangrenous intestines -- and I was back in Connecticut, this time with Lucy. We visited Mama in the hospital and helped Daddy settle into his nursing home, bringing him fresh socks and pajamas from a nearby five and dime. A year later Lucy killed herself. Two months later, Daddy died. Two years later, my father-in-law died. Two months later, my mother died. Count 'em: Four major funerals in 26 months.

After a while, grief becomes a habit. Coping becomes one's modus operandi -- a constant sorting of emotions, legalities, lost days and dusty relics. In my attic are too many boxes of dead people's things. In my home are too many inherited furnishings: a sofa, a loveseat, chairs, a stereo, two televisions, two secretaries, a couple of wardrobes, a round maple table and the dining room table where the Biancollis ate Thanksgiving turkey and I scrawled through many a semicolonic English essay. "Everything we own comes from a dead person," observed my husband one day, and we laughed at the truth of it. At one point we owned two cars passed down from dead people; to this day Chris and I walk around in a couple of Lucy's sweatshirts. After my mother died we rented out her chummy ranch house, and Chris built a Musée Biancolli in the basement: a storage room for every last stick of furniture, sheet of music, scrap of writing and stack of Polaroids that we couldn't squeeze into our home in Albany. Most families have a self-appointed archivist, someone who saves letters and keeps notebooks and hoards cracked snapshots in a shoebox -- but few are as unwitting, or as haphazard, as I am. Here walks the last living member of an obscure tribe of packrats. Allow me introduce myself: I am the Most High Keeper of the Stuff.

I hope, someday, my children will know what it means to be a Biancolli. They have an inkling now, I think -- they've figured out already that the Biancollis were above all entertaining, and hardly a day passes without one of them clamoring for a story. "Tell us about Aunt Lucy and the poopy cookies!" they demand. Or, "Tell the one about Grandpa Louis and the bananas!" Or, "Grandpa Louis' magic pocket! Grandma Jeanne's frozen chicken! Aunt Lucy's wacky hair!" Or simply: "Tell us a funny story about your family -- ONE WE HAVEN'T HEARD!" Sometimes I'm tempted to start making them up. Twelve times a day we pass photos of Louis and Lucy and Jeanne on the landing, and periodically I pause to quiz the kids: Do you know who this is? Do you know where this was?

Yeah, yeah, Mommy -- we know. You told us already. We know.

Some years ago, after Madeleine learned to talk, I made up words for a boppy tune Mama and Daddy had written for us as children -- "The Happy Song," I called it back then. It's chipper little ditty, Vaudevillian in its innocence, major key all the way. I wrote chipper little lyrics to go along.

> B-B-B-B is for Biancolli
> I-I-I-I is for Italian roots
> A-A-A-A is for Amy the youngest
> N-N-N-N is for No one but Jeanne
> C-C-C-C is for cozy Connecticut
> O-O-O-Oh, do you hear the music play?
> L-L-L-L is for Lucy and
> L is for Louis and
> I is for I love you!

My children sing this song -- hum it, ask me to sing it, hear me pick it out on the piano, pick it out themselves. It tickles me to hear them. I think: They know about the Biancollis. They're Biancollis themselves. I think: Maybe the dead aren't lost forever. Maybe while we speak of them, they aren't lost at all.

Unlike their reformed-atheistic convert of a mom, my kids are cradle Catholics. They believe in a God, in an afterlife. They're convinced that Grandma Jeanne and Grandpa Louis and Aunt Lucy know them and love them and wait, hovering in their otherworldly jet-packs, until we're all united some day. "We have too many friends in Heaven," Madeleine complained one day after a woman we knew, a great one, died of cancer. Then we lost another friend: a new mother who wouldn't be around to watch her baby grow. But she'll see her child from Heaven, Chris assured the girls. Madeleine replied: "And you can see more clearly from Heaven."

My daydreams, these days, are so mundane. Gone are the reveries of running for president while writing best-selling murder mysteries and reporting for the CBS Evening News from the roiling surface of Jupiter in a pressurized suit of my own invention. These days I fantasize about hugging my parents. I think about

Madeleine's Russian playmates and the words of friendship Daddy would have spoken to them in their native tongue. Most of all, I like to imagine what might have been had Lucy lived to take my kids for a walk -- maybe they'd return with ice cream cones, or a couple of library books, or daisies. It's a nice illusion, only passingly bathetic, until I remember that Lucy's suicide prompted me to get pregnant to begin with: If she hadn't died, Madeleine, Mitchell and Jeanne might not exist. I might have *other children*, an unfathomable thought for a parent, or I might have none at all. The bass-ackwards beauty of this world is its insistence on the goodness of bad things -- its serial transference of death to life, of calamity to joy. I can mourn Lucy's death, but I can't forsake the day it happened. I can't change it and I wouldn't, given the chance, nor would I bump back the clock to bring back Mama and Daddy. I thank them and God for what they gave me, and I rejoice in the time we shared, but I've no desire to preserve them as they were or me as I was. For that I'd need formaldehyde.

The truth of this came home to me recently in an instant of such abrupt clarity that I dare call it epiphany. There I was, lying in bed with a kidney infection and a fever of 103.3, thinking about this book. I was thinking about my persistent fear of being a Biancolli, my sense that I'm somehow toxic. I was thinking my back hurt and I felt like throwing up and I couldn't stop shaking and where the hell was Chris with that Cipro prescription. I was thinking about all the discomfort and illness in life, all of the fragility and darkness. All of the death.

Then it hit me, this understanding announced by tears. I realized in a flash that the blackest moments in my family's life were in fact the brightest, for they were the moments that opened us all to the unblinking light of God. At once I recognized not just the gift of Lucy's life and Mama's and Daddy's, but the gift of their illnesses and deaths -- gifts of insight, or grace. In that one moment even the horror of Lucy's suicide and Daddy's attempt appeared as glimpses of divinity from the same: Suddenly I could picture only the beauty of life (mine, theirs, ours) and the tight, continuous weave binding this world to the next one. Indeed it struck me as all one world. All one life. A quilt of boundless color and dimension, diminished only by our own confused reluctance to see it. In an instant that I remember but expect never to repeat, I saw.

For so long I had imagined my family being stalked by Death. I had thought of our difficulties as brushes with doom. I was wrong: They were brushes dwith eternity. And from the start, we were stalked by God.

*****

Someday, I hope, my kids will read this thing I've written and understand that it's written with love -- love for them, love for the dead. I'd like my children to know how their family lived and found God and died, all with inexhaustible spirit. More than that, I'd like them to feel an inviolable link with the past, not as runners in a long genetic relay but as luminous birds that rise from the pyres of madness. The myth of the Phoenix is a tale of suicide, after all. But it is also a tale of life redeemed, of irrational hope, of flames that purify and wounds that salve and the wild-blind faith that sends us to our deaths. My children live because my parents and sister died. Because my parents and sister suffered. Because my parents and sister saw what was coming and stretched out their wings and flew. They were crazy enough to spot the way, and crazy enough to get there.

Acknowledgments

The author would like to thank every last soul who read this book and believed in it and said so. Dan and Pat and Jeanette and Alicia and Pam and Susi and Sue and Tamar and Bev and Willie and Fourgie and Uncle Allie and Aunt Charlotte and Jane and Celina, thank you. My beloved Chris, thank you, for all of it: You never gave up, even when I did. Madeleine, Jeanne and Mitchell, thank you for being so happy and loud. Margaret, thank you for sharing your father with me. Dan and Louise, thank you for taking a good hard crack at it. Family, friends, Ringwalds, Richardsons, Grove Avenue Gang: Thanks. Thank you, God, and thank God for you all.

www.ingramcontent.com/pod-product-compliance
Lightning Source LLC
Chambersburg PA
CBHW020433290526
45785CB00002B/821